If I'm Created *in God's Image*

Why Does It Hurt to Look in the Mirror?

A TRUE VIEW OF YOU

by Stanley C. Baldwin

Aglow Publications

A Ministry of Women's Aglow Fellowship, Int'l.
P.O. Box 1548
Lynnwood, WA 98046-1558
USA

To
Kathy Holland
Krystal Brown
Karen Kraus
my little sweethearts,
now grown-up women of God

Cover design by David Marty

Unless otherwise noted, all scripture quotations in this publication are from the Holy Bible, New International Version. Copyright 1973, 1978, 1984, International Bible Society. Other versions are abbreviated as follows: TLB (The Living Bible), Beck (The New Testament in the Language of Today), KJV (King James Version).

ISBN 0-932305-76-8

Contents

PART IV
Performance Counts

Part I

A True View of You

Introduction

"This could confuse some of our people," a pastor told me, referring to my seminar flyer.

"We have been teaching them for years to renounce self, that the self-life is base and sinful. Now you want to tell them how to 'like themselves, free themselves, and develop their potential.' You should avoid that kind of language because it smacks of humanism and runs counter to the biblical description of mankind."

I was somewhat intimidated. I knew the problem of low self-esteem existed, but I had felt that people simply needed to be re-educated a bit. They needed to understand that the self is not essentially evil, though the word has sometimes carried that connotation. But now I was wondering. If the Bible consistently used the term in a negative sense. . . .

When I got home, I dug out my Young's Concordance. Did I get an education! I discovered that the Bible does not use the

9

word *self* the negative way the pastor said it did. The Bible does not talk about *self* as an entity in the way it sometimes talks about the *flesh*—as the unregenerate, base element in man. *Self* is mostly used in a morally neutral sense as in the reflexive pronouns (myself, himself, yourself). Exceptions to this usage are in passages such as Titus 1:7 and 2 Peter 2:10, where Scripture warns against being self-willed, otherwise translated headstrong, overbearing, or arrogant.

If, then, Christians have a negative concept of the word *self*, it is because they have been mistaught. It is time for those who have mistakenly made *self* synonymous with *the flesh* to correct their error.

/ Apart from the connotations of the word *self*, however, Christians are properly concerned about an over-emphasis on man, his needs, and the fulfillment of those needs. Man tends to be egocentric. That is his basic sin—he is self-centered instead of God-centered. Too much talk about a good self-image, freeing oneself, and developing one's potential may simply cater to man's egocentric bent; God and Christ need to be kept central in our teaching and in our thinking.

The truth is, however, that Christianity concerns God and man. Healthy, correct concepts about both are essential. One can become unbalanced when focusing just on God, as the following sometimes-popular poem illustrates:

Oh, the bitter pain and sorrow
That a time could ever be
When I proudly said to Jesus,
"All of self, and none of Thee."
Yet He found me; I beheld Him
Bleeding on the accursed tree;
And my wistful heart said faintly,
"Some of self, and some of Thee."
Day by day His tender mercy,
Healing, helping, full and free,
Brought me lower, while I whispered,

"Less of self, and more of Thee!"
Higher than the highest heavens,
Deeper than the deepest sea,
"Lord, Thy love at last has conquered;
None of self and all of Thee!"

Theodore Monod

The poem, while beautifully reflective of a growing conse-cration, has problems. First, it uses the word *self* in a negative, contrary-to-God sense, typical of some Christians, but not typi-cal of Scripture. Second, if taken literally, the poem urges an extreme renunciation of the self which is more consistent with Hindu theology than with Christianity. If Monod's final prayer were granted, no person would be left to glorify or enjoy God.

Actually, those who shrink from a positive use of the word *self* are not all that God-centered. Even their evangelism is usually ego-centered. They seldom urge people to be born again in order to glorify God. No, they tell people it's either be converted or be lost. The very expression *saved* is man-cen-tered. After all, it's not God who is being saved; it is man. I am in no way deprecating the salvation message. I'm only pointing out the self-interest upon which it is based.

Christian music reflects this same self-interest. I grew up in a fundamentalist church. Self was equivalent to sin. Nevertheless, our leaders taught us to sing heartily:

If you want joy, real joy, wonderful joy;
Let Jesus come into your heart.[1]

It's hard to imagine a more unabashed appeal to self-interest. There's no concern for the glory of God here. No ethical or moral principle is advanced. It's simply advice on how to get the joy you want, through Jesus.

In fact, the music of the church probably appeals to self-interest more often than not.

"What a Friend We Have in Jesus!" Why is he such a good

11

friend? "All of our sins and griefs to bear!"

"Trust and Obey." Why? "For there's no other way *to be happy* in Jesus."

"Rock of Ages." What about it? "Let me hide myself in Thee."

"The Old Rugged Cross." Ah, at last, a song centering on the redemptive work of our Lord Jesus Christ. Yes, but even here we end up singing, "I will cling to the old rugged cross, and *exchange it someday for a crown.*"

Don't misunderstand. I'm not finding fault with the songs. I'm only pointing out that Christianity is not anti-self, and we ought not reject psychological teaching consistent with Scripture simply because we have an unfounded emotional reaction against the term *self* or because we imagine the best Christianity to be selfless.

Otherwise, we had better rewrite the hymns of the church. But that would not solve the self-interest problem, for as it turns out, even the Bible appeals to us on that level.

"Believe in the Lord Jesus." Why? "And you will be saved" (Acts 16:31).

"Do not judge." Why? "Or you too will be judged" (Matt. 7:1).

Jesus said to one man, "If you want to be perfect, go, sell your possessions and give to the poor, and *you will have treasure in heaven*" (Matt. 19:21, italics added).

"Let us not become weary in doing good." Why? Because doing good is the Christian way to live? No. "For at the proper time *we will reap* a harvest if we do not give up" (Gal. 6:9, italics added).

One last example: "Do not let this Book of the Law depart from your mouth; meditate on it day and night, so that you may be careful to do everything written in it. Then *you will be prosperous, and successful*" (Josh. 1:8, italics added).

Christianity is not a religion aimed at swallowing up the individual in the essence of God as the rivers are lost in the sea. To the contrary, self-realization harmonizes with the teaching of the Bible much better than self-abnegation. Why do we hesitate to say so?

What is the Bible all about? What is the nature of Christianity? If we say it is about God and his glory we are right, but we have not said enough. It is also about man as a creature of God and his needs as they are met by God's loving providence. The Bible teaches God can be known and loved and served by man.

Humanism, on the other hand, is "a philosophy that asserts the dignity and worth of man and his capacity for self-realization through reason and that often rejects supernaturalism" (Webster).

If we urge people to find self-realization through responding to God, we certainly are not embracing a humanism that "rejects supernaturalism." We may be accused of promoting "theistic humanism," I suppose, but if we are, so does the Bible.

With these thoughts in mind, I offer to the community of believers—and to any others—this book. I am not a psychologist and I do not write from that viewpoint. What I mean to do is apply the principles of Scripture to some of the psychological teachings of our day and to the human condition as I observe it. Particularly, I have applied biblical principles to the question of how we should see ourselves.

If I seem to have come down on a positive, self-realization note, so much the better. I am not likely to promise more in this regard than the Scripture warrants. How could I when "all things are yours, whether Paul or Apollos or Cephas or the world or life or death or the present or the future—all are yours, and you are of Christ, and Christ is of God" (1 Cor. 3:21-23)?

1

...

Because You Laugh, Should I Feel Funny?

I have a certain pair of shoes that are tricky to walk in. The soles are corrugated and thicker at the instep than anywhere else. Ordinarily, I can walk fine in them, but occasionally if I am in a hurry that thick instep trips me up. I have to be fast on my feet to keep from falling.

I was all dressed up one day and crossing an intersection in Salem, Oregon, on my way to visit a pastor. In the middle of the intersection, as I was hurrying to make the light, my shoes did their thing. I wasn't nimble enough to recover—down I went!

Talk about embarrassed! You'd have thought I had done something shameful the way I scrambled to my feet and avoided looking around at anyone who might be watching. I quickly brushed myself off and hurried on as though nothing had happened, ignoring the painful bruise on my elbow that I would have stopped to examine had I been in private.

Why did I behave that way? I had done nothing of which to

be ashamed.

Though I didn't analyze my feelings at the time, it is clear on reflection that my distress was due to viewing myself from another's perspective. I was an object of amusement, a spectacle to be laughed at, a clumsy oaf.

Why do I tell you this? First, though I have often spoken and written about how to have a healthy self-image, I am not immune to the negative influence of others myself. Accordingly, you will find no easy once-for-all solutions to the problem in this book. Instead, we will explore solid biblical principles that work for me when I apply them and that can work for you as well.

Second, I recount the tricky-shoe episode because although it was a trivial incident, analyzing the nature of embarrassment is not so trivial.

Embarrassment reflects the fact that our view of ourselves is influenced by others' views of us. People frequently affect the way we think about ourselves.

Longshoreman philosopher Eric Hoffer expressed the concept as follows: "It is thus with most of us: we are what other people say we are. We know ourselves chiefly by hearsay."

When people give us negative feedback, we internalize it and think or feel badly about ourselves. When they affirm us, we feel good and inwardly applaud ourselves.

My embarrassment over falling illustrates the operation of negative feedback. An example of the positive variety is the Special Olympics, a nationwide program of athletic events for retarded people.

Every entrant in the Special Olympics is awarded a ribbon, regardless of how he or she places in the competition. Each is also greeted at the finish line by "huggers and back-slappers" who praise the person's efforts to the cheering of the crowd.

The result is smiles and shining eyes, the proud wearing of ribbons, joy on the faces and in the hearts of the athletes.

Why?

Not because they have outdone someone else, but because

they see themselves through the eyes of others as deserving praise and recognition.

Some literature in philosophy and psychology maintains that *all* self-awareness depends on and is created by our interaction with others. While that could be debated, much of our self-concept seems clearly conditioned by such feedback.

DAMAGING DISTORTIONS

The difficulty with this feedback system of self-evalution is that it subjects us to distortions of reality in the way we see ourselves. Three major factors are at work.

First, others do not always perceive us correctly. They often misunderstand our actions and misread our intent. Seeing our shyness as aloofness, they may call us proud. Reading our eagerness as arrogance, they may try to cut us down to size. Then, too, others have emotional needs and problems of their own that may lead them to judge us unfairly.

Second, we may misinterpret what others say and do. For example, if we are over-sensitive, any correction or criticism may be taken as a personal insult, a message that we are not acceptable.

Third, the values by which we are rated may be far astray from the mark. One cannot live uprightly in this perverse world without being put down for it by someone. As the Scripture says, "They think it strange that you do not plunge with them into the same flood of dissipation, and they heap abuse on you" (1 Pet. 4:4).

Sometimes the world's distorted evaluation of us is apparent, as was the case with my shame over tripping in public. Intellectually, I knew that falling down was nothing against me. Even so, I was shaken emotionally almost as much as if I had performed a shameful act.

What would be one's trauma, then, if both intellectually and emotionally one accepted a distorted view from the world? One could be severely damaged.

17

Jill was eleven years old and slightly plump when a teacher commented about her roly poly shape. At home that night, Jill's mirror told her the teacher was right—even too kind. She was worse than chubby, she told herself. She was ugly and fat.

The horror of her condition burned itself into Jill's mind. She began to eat less but without immediate effect, of course. The image staring back at her from the mirror still looked repulsive. Soon her excess flesh became an obsession to Jill.

Today, at age sixteen, Jill weighs eighty-seven pounds and suffers from anorexia nervosa, a mental illness marked by loss of appetite and inability to keep food down. Death by starvation is possible. While Jill's disease cannot be specifically attributed to her neuroses about being overweight, one might certainly suspect a connection.

No rational appeal to Jill can help her. Just as I knew I had done nothing shameful when I fell in public, Jill "knows" she is not overweight. And just as my knowledge did not keep me from feeling embarrassed, Jill's knowledge does not keep her from feeling as if she is fat.

In a thousand subtle and not-so-subtle ways, people are damaged by the world's distorted views of them. To expose and counteract these errors is the purpose of this book.

HOW CAN WE GET AN UNDISTORTED VIEW OF OURSELVES?

A familiar Scripture says, "Do not conform any longer to the pattern of this world, but be transformed by the renewing of your mind" (Rom. 12:2). This principle is appropriately applied to many areas of the Christian life. What most of us fail to realize is that it applies in its immediate context to the issue raised here—namely, the need to see ourselves correctly instead of as the world sees us.

Observe. Immediately after telling us not to conform to the world but to be transformed by a renewed mind, the Scripture says "For by the grace given to me I say to every one of you: Do not think of yourself more highly than you ought, but rather think of yourself with sober judgment, in accordance with the measure of faith God has given you"(Rom. 12:3).

What is the subject under discussion? How we are to think of ourselves.

We need to make one critical preliminary observation at this point. According to this Scripture, it is not only permissible but desirable to "think of yourself."

Some say otherwise. Some tell us we must forget ourselves; we must not think of ourselves at all. Such teaching is an understandable reaction to the "me first" or "me only" attitude of the present generation. It is also an accepted, traditional way of thinking in evangelical circles.

However, it does not square with Scripture. The Bible does not say: "Do not think of yourselves more highly than you ought *but rather forget yourself.*" No, it says: "Do not think of yourself more highly than you ought, but rather think of yourself with sober judgment."

Certainly, to be preoccupied with thoughts of ourselves is not healthy. On the other hand, some kind of self-concept is not only proper but inescapable. As self-conscious beings, aware of our own existence, we cannot help having some underlying assumptions about ourselves.

It is critical that our underlying assumptions be correct because everything we do or say flows from what we are or think we are.

Scripture says our self-concept should be based on "sober judgment." The word *sober* could be translated "sound-minded" or "sane." We are called to a sane self-evaluation.

What is likely to be the case instead? We are likely to be unsound in our self-evaluation, too much influenced by the world.

When we are told not to be conformed to the world in this area, we are assigned quite a task since so much of self-evaluation originates from one's interaction with others. We, by contrast, are told to be transformed by a renewed mind. Our self-concept must originate from God, his Word, and his Spirit dwelling within us, not from the world.

It's a profound difference, but doing what God says here is not necessarily difficult. Many Christians can testify that just such a thing is happening in their lives. Though they have at times been saddled with a world-conditioned view of themselves, the Spirit of God has used the Word of God to transform their thinking—and as a result, their lives.

Jerry Cook's experience is typical. He writes:

> I lived a lot of my life trying to get God to accept me. I didn't like me very well. I was too short. My ears were too big. I wasn't put together the way I thought best.
>
> I was crossing the street in Seattle one day when the Lord spoke to me clearly, "Jerry, why don't you quit trying to be a Christian? You are one. You are accepted in the Beloved." I did not even know that last phrase was in the Bible.
>
> Three days later, I was lying on my bed in the room I was renting near the college. I opened my Bible to Ephesians, chapter 1, and began reading. When I reached the sixth verse, it jumped on me like a thing alive—I am "accepted in the beloved" (KJV).
>
> That experience totally changed my life. Suddenly I wasn't trying to get God to like me anymore. He had liked me all the time.[1]

So far we have said three important things.

1. Our self-concept is largely determined by the attitude of others (our world) toward us.

2. The world's judgments of us are unreliable and often wrong.

3. A new, correct, and liberating way of thinking about ourselves can come to us from God.

In succeeding chapters, we will observe some ways these principles work in our lives.

TIME TO CONSIDER

1. How comfortable do you feel discussing yourself—your weaknesses and your strengths? Is it easier for you to discuss one than the other? On a scale of one to ten, with one being extremely uneasy and ten being totally comfortable, how well do you take criticism? How well do you take compliments?

2. Are you more or less comfortable with yourself now than you were five years ago? If your comfort with yourself has changed, what do you think accounts for it?

3. Would you be skeptical about a person who claims, "I don't care what anyone thinks or says about me?" Why or why not?

4. When a person you respect criticizes you, are you more likely to:
   a. be upset and hurt
   b. calmly weigh the merits of criticism
   c. ignore it

What should be your reaction? When you do react inappropriately, what is the cause?

2

...

Seeing Ourselves as God Sees Us

Vain people who spend their time looking into mirrors have not fared well in the history of literature. One of the oldest vanity stories comes from Greek mythology and concerns a handsome young man named Narcissus.

Many women fell in love with Narcissus. One named Echo loved him so much that she pined away until nothing was left of her but her voice. Narcissus did not return Echo's love or the love of the other women who admired him. He had once seen his handsome face mirrored in a pool of water, had fallen in love with his own reflection, and could thereafter love no one but himself.

From this myth comes the word *narcissism*, which means excessive admiration of or fascination with oneself.

Another story in which a mirror plays a large part is "Snow White and the Seven Dwarfs." Snow White's wicked step-mother loved to gaze into her mirror and hear it tell her she was the fairest person in the land. When the mirror began to say Snow White was fairest instead, the stepmother wanted to kill Snow White to eliminate her as a rival.

These stories warn against being obsessed with our appearance. Vanity is destructive both to vain people (like Narcissus) and to those unfortunate enough to be involved with a vain person (such as Snow White).

Still, looking at yourself in a mirror is not all bad. Most of us do so every time we leave our homes. Women carry a mirror with them in their purses to check their appearance while away from home.

MIRRORS OF THE SOUL

We also have mirrors for our personalities. As stated in the previous chapter, we tend to see ourselves as others see us. In other words, our world serves as our mirror, indicating that we are OK or not OK, interesting or uninteresting, worthwhile or not worthwhile, and so on.

The problem is that these reflections can be and often are distorted. It reminds me of Jantzen Beach, an amusement park of my youth. Jantzen Beach had a fun house with a hall of mirrors. How we laughed at the way those mirrors made us look. One made me short and fat, the next tall and thin. One reflected a tall, thin face and a short, fat body, while another made me look like a crooked man who walked a crooked mile.

The hall of mirrors was a fun place to visit. You wouldn't want to live there, though. How would you ever know what you really looked like?

Suppose for a moment you lived in a house with only the short, fat mirror. How could you escape seeing yourself as short and fat? In time, you would grow so accustomed to that image that even if you gazed on a true reflection of yourself, you would discount it as the unrepresentative one.

Some people live with similar psychological distortions. Their milieu reflects an image that is one-sided and false. All of

24

us live in a hall of mirrors or at least pass through one regularly, for our world reflects all kinds of distorted images of us.

No wonder people are confused about their identities. Too often they receive conflicting information.

As I recall, the hall of mirrors at Jantzen Beach had one unique mirror that a person came to last. It gave a true and undistorted reflection of the person standing before it. It kind of restored your sanity—reminded you of what you actually looked like and reassured you that all the grotesque distortions were unreal.

GOD'S TRUE MIRROR

We have available to us a true and undistorted mirror in which we may see ourselves. That mirror is the Bible. We read:

Do not merely listen to the word, and so deceive your-selves. Do what it says. Anyone who listens to the word but does not do what it says is like a man who looks at his face in a mirror and, after looking at himself, goes away and immediately forgets what he looks like. But the man who looks intently into the perfect law that gives freedom, and continues to do this, not forgetting what he has heard, but doing it—he will be blessed in what he does (James 1:22-25).

The Word of God reflects a true image of us. But we must see this true reflection more than once in a while to correct the confusion that comes from continually passing through the hall of mirrors. We must look often enough and long enough so that we remember what we look like.

If you look into God's Word sufficiently, you will know, for example, that the world's praise for some conspicuous achieve-ment does not mean you are a Superior Person. You will also know that the world's criticism, though it comes in a hundred forms, does not mean you are an Inferior Person.

Without God's mirror, though, we are likely to hold both of the above illusions simultaneously, even though that doesn't make sense. That is, a person can be both proud and self-despising at the same time. This is not only possible but common.

Here's how it works. Lack of self-esteem is painful and causes us to grasp for something to compensate, to ease the pain of feeling insignificant or unworthy. We fight against whatever aggravates our condition and reflects on us adversely. We become over-sensitive, thin-skinned, defensive. We desperately latch on to whatever makes us look good. We become proud, vain, and critical of others. In chapter four we will see some examples of how this plays out in people's lives.

WHAT GOD'S MIRROR SHOWS

James writes that one needs to look "intently into the perfect law that gives freedom" and continue to do this, "not forgetting" (1:25) in order to truly see and know what one is like. We need to continue looking our entire lives to get and keep the complete picture. Let's observe features that stand out prominently in the divine reflection of who we are.

1. *We are made in God's image.*

Scripture says, "God created man in his own image" (Gen. 1:27). The entire account of God's early dealing with man emphasizes our unique value. Jerry Cook puts it this way:

Think about it. When man fell, God did not choose to get rid of him and make a new creature. That might have been a more efficient way, and certainly a less painful way, for God to handle the whole business. 'Chuck this wretch; let's start all over. This loser can incinerate along with the planet.' But, no, God chose to let the planet die, which it will, but save the race. And he will give us a new earth on which to live.[1]

26

That's a profound truth and it says volumes about the intrinsic value of human beings. God established our value in the beginning. God did not make human beings the same way he made everything else. The rest of creation God spoke into existence. He uttered the word and, boom, it was there. Not so with man. God *formed* man out of the dust of the earth. He took a rib from man and *formed* the woman (see Genesis 2:7,22).

> We, then, are a contemplated creation. We were in the mind of God, and he specifically formed us with his hand. That's not true of any other animal, plant, or thing on earth.[2]

God's Word consistently reflects man as being a special creature made in the divine image. What a significant thing that is to know and believe!

Our unbelieving friends miss this truth. They live without ultimate meaning, purpose, or dignity because they see themselves only as the chance products of mindless evolution. Though they hold this gloomy concept of the human race, unbelievers still grope for some reason for living, of course, because they need it. But they have no logical basis either for wanting self-esteem or obtaining it.

We who know God are not so forlorn. We know we are not just dirt but are made in God's image. Yet while unbelievers grope for a sense of worth while having no basis for it, we have the basis but often fail to realize the implications of what we say we believe.

We are victimized by a variety of circumstances, lied to, defrauded, and led away from the wonderful but staggering truth of Scripture that we are made in God's image.

I wonder if something like that happened to Eve. The serpent suggested that by eating the forbidden fruit she could become "like God" (see Genesis 3:5). But she was already like God, lovingly formed in his image. Was Eve unaware of her divine likeness, somehow already beguiled by Satan? Why else would she have been tempted to gain by disobedience what she already had by God's great love?

To the degree that you have looked into God's mirror and know who you are, to that degree you are invulnerable to the temptation to try to become someone or to prove you are someone.

Compare Jesus' and Eve's response to the same situation. Eve fell when Satan offered to make her like God. When Satan offered Jesus power over the kingdoms of this world (God-like power), he had no success (see Matthew 4:8-10). Jesus knew he was already heir to all the kingdoms of this world.

Jesus did not have to grasp for significance to feel secure about his worth and identity. He had no need to jump from a pinnacle of the temple to prove himself. The apostle Paul describes Jesus' attitude as follows: "Who, being in very nature God, did not consider equality with God something to be grasped, but made himself nothing, taking the very nature of a servant" (Phil. 2:6,7).

Jesus could perform menial tasks, such as washing his disciples' feet, and not feel demeaned by it because he knew his identity. He was not one whit less the eternal Son of God draped in a towel washing feet than when he rode as a king into Jerusalem while the crowd sang hosanna.

Do you long to feel secure in who you are with no need to prove anything to anybody? Do you wish you could genuinely serve others from the heart with no hidden agenda of self-seeking?

You will be able to do these things when the truth sinks in and you realize who you are in Christ. It starts with grasping that you are one of the unique creatures, called a human, whom God *made in his own image.*

2. *We are personally important to God.*

Jesus said, "Are not five sparrows sold for two pennies? Yet not one of them is forgotten by God. Indeed, the very hairs of your head are all numbered. Don't be afraid; you are worth more than many sparrows" (Luke 12:6,7).

Jesus made it clear that we are valuable to God and a sense of value is something we all need. Even my small grandchildren are forever coming to me for recognition. "Look, Grandpa, see what I made." Or "Look, Grandpa, see what I can do."

Currently, the youngest is so proud of her latest achievement that she spontaneously thanks God every night in her prayers for her potty-chair.

We all reach for significance but not always in constructive ways. Some knock themselves out to reach impressive heights. Some try to associate themselves with great people or great causes. Some seek leadership by condemning everyone else. Some choose a path of domination, seeking stature by controlling those around them. A few kill somebody famous and grab headlines.

The deep, inner deficit in our feeling of significance that gives rise to these destructive lifestyles is evidence of world conformity. The renewed mind, by contrast, thinks as Jesus said we should. "Don't be afraid," he said. We can relax and be secure in our standing with him.

"You are worth more than many sparrows," he said. We need not feel driven to establish our value for he has already conferred worth upon us.

We need only make ourselves available to him who says, "I know the plans I have for you . . . plans to prosper you and not to harm you, plans to give you hope and a future" (Jer. 29:11).

Think of it! God has plans for you. It's as if you received a personal message:

Dear Child: Relax. You matter to me. I have good plans for you. And I never forget you for a moment.

(signed) God

David described God's personal concern for him this way, "How precious it is, Lord, to realize that you are thinking about me constantly! I can't even count how many times a day your thoughts turn towards me. And when I waken in the morning, you are still thinking of me!" (Ps. 139:17,18 TLB).

The mirror of God's Word reveals clearly that we are each

29

personally important to him.

3. *We are God's inheritance.*

Paul prayed that believers might be enlightened in order to know "the riches of his glorious inheritance in the saints" (see Ephesians 1:18). This passage is not talking about *our* inheritance—what we have in Christ. It is talking about *God's* inheritance—what he has in us. His inheritance in us is rich and glorious.

Inheritances disappoint many people who hope to receive much and get little. They judge their inheritance as poor and miserable. God's inheritance is *us*, and he is not complaining. He doesn't view us as a poor and miserable inheritance but a rich and glorious one.

The prophet Isaiah, looking ahead to the great sacrifice of the cross, wrote concerning the Messiah, "He shall see of the travail of his soul, and shall be satisfied: by his knowledge shall my righteous servant justify many; for he shall bear their iniquities" (Isa. 53:11, KJV).

Jesus paid a great price to redeem us to himself, but what is staggering is that he is satisfied with his purchase!

Have you ever experienced "buyer's remorse"? You bought something and then had troubling second thoughts. The actual possession of the item was not nearly so grand as you imagined, and you realized you paid too much. "Why, oh why, did I buy this?" you groaned.

This *isn't* how Jesus feels about you. He knew what he was doing, and he is not sorry he did it.

A good question for determining the value of anything is this: How much would a knowledgeable person be willing to pay for this? Our Lord, who knows us best, values us enough to pay the price of the cross that we might belong to him. How beautiful we become, despite the ugliness Satan has brought into our lives, when we see ourselves in the mirror of God's Word!

At grand social events guests are announced as they enter. They are presented to the roomful of important people. If you ever have the privilege to meet royalty, you will be presented to the king or queen as the case may be.

How do you envision the moment when you at last come into the majestic presence of God? Jude describes Jesus as follows: "To him who is able to keep you from falling and to present you before his glorious presence without fault and with great joy" (Jude 24).

Jude says we are going to be presented to God. It is the language of formal recognition. The one who will present us is Jesus Christ. Jesus is not going to sneak us into some back door of heaven, ashamed to be seen with us. We are not going to slip in with a crowd either, privileged to be one of an accepted group but personally unworthy and ignored.

Jesus will march us right into the glorious presence of God and present us to the Father. Know how he will feel as he introduces us? He will experience "great joy."

Sometimes on earth we are rejected or overlooked, slighted or ignored. At such times this hall of mirrors through which we are passing doesn't make us look very good. The true mirror of God's Word shows a different and wondrously better reflection, of which we have seen only a part. Which mirror will you use?

TIME TO CONSIDER

1. Will a person usually find that her self-concept problems disappear once she knows scriptural solutions? Why or why not? How do the verbs in James 1:25 (*looks intently, continues, not forgetting*) apply here?

2. What do you think of God? How impressed are you with the fact that you are created in God's image? How does your response compare with David's in Psalm 8?

3. We need to feel we have significance, that our existence matters. Select one verse from the following scriptures and explain how it communicates that you are significant to God: Psalm 139:14-18; Isaiah 66:1,2; Jeremiah 29:11; Luke 12:6,7.

Memorize the verse.

4. According to Ephesians 1:18, what body of people does God consider his rich and glorious inheritance? How does this fact affect your view of yourself? How does it affect your view of other Christians, including those who are lightly regarded?

5. Imagine how you will feel when Jesus, with great joy, presents you faultless to God (Jude 24). How will that compare with other peak experiences of your life? How does your knowledge of this future event affect your life now?

3
...

To the
"Truly Inferior"

I was in Eugene, Oregon, conducting a "Take Charge of Your Life" seminar on how to "like yourself, free yourself, and develop your potential." A young man approached me during a break. "What you say is all well and good," he remarked, "for those who have lots of potential but a low self-image. But some of us don't just *feel* inferior; we *are* inferior."

If you are like that young man, you desperately need to hear what God has to say on inferiority. The natural human inclination is to get things out of balance one way or another.

Sober judgment—sane self-evaluation—requires that we see our limitations, our weaknesses, and our failings as well as our strengths. Both are a part of the true picture.

At one time, church leaders sounded forth loud and clear the dangers of pride. Some still do. People must be warned from thinking too highly of themselves.

In many churches today, however, the pendulum has swung

to the opposite extreme. The teaching is geared totally toward building self-esteem. People must be warned from thinking too lowly of themselves.

Some teaching goes even further. It says that we are such wonderful people that we can do anything on which we set our minds. All we need is the faith and courage to venture out, and God will surely bring us through to glorious and wonderful triumph. Few say it in those words, but that is what is sometimes perceived.

Such was the case with the "truly inferior" young man in Eugene who had a heart-rending story to tell. As a result of hearing various positive thinking, you-can-do-whatever-you-set-your-mind-on, human potential presentations, he confidently launched his own business. When things didn't work out, he ran through the litany: keep faith, don't give up, you can do it if you believe you can.

The young man stubbornly pursued his dream, sacrificing everything, until his wife took their children and left him. He became hopelessly in debt, and the business dwindled to nothing.

Now I was seeing him a couple of years later. He was working at a menial job, had remarried, and was beginning to fellowship with God's people again. He was also wounded and scarred. He felt he had been misled by those who encouraged him to assume that anyone has what it takes to achieve his dreams if he but believes in himself.

"Remember," he told me, "some of us don't just feel inferior; we *are* inferior."

If you feel inferior or if you "are inferior," you need to consider four important facts about inferiority.

1. *Everyone Is Inferior in Some Ways*

Ludwig von Beethoven had a pockmarked face, and his front teeth protruded. His hair was unruly, and he looked like he was always scowling. His mother died when he was sixteen, and his father was a drunk. Ludwig had a violent temper and was a poor manager of money. Worst of all for a musician and composer, he began going deaf at age thirty. Yet he was one of the greatest composers of all time, with much of his best work created after he had totally lost his hearing.

The apostle Paul was personally unattractive. People said his bodily presence was "unimpressive" and his speech contemptible (see 2 Corinthians 10:10). Not very promising traits for a preacher. Yet Paul changed the history of the world through his preaching and writing.

Napoleon was a sawed-off runt so short even his friends called him "Little Corporal."

Abraham Lincoln was physically ugly, with a tall, gangly build, a big nose, and a wart on his craggy face.

Franklin D. Roosevelt was crippled.

Albert Einstein was a failure in school.

Even Jesus Christ came from a despised town so that people said of him, "Can any good thing come out of Nazarath?" He was also subject to rumors of a dishonorable parentage.

When we say we are inferior, what do we actually mean? Usually we mean that in certain ways other people excel us. It is a comparison game, and how we come out depends on which trait we choose to compare. In some ways, most other people excel you. In some ways, you probably excel most other people.

Judging oneself either inferior or superior is often subjective. For example, a small man may feel inferior and may be referred to by others as a shrimp or peewee. But what objective disadvantages has he? Some perhaps, but he also has advantages. Usually the compact physiology of a small man makes for better health than does the stretched-out body of a large person. In fact, tall men are almost notorious for having bad backs.

Nevertheless, let us acknowledge that some people are generally inferior to most others physically, mentally, and in talents. This brings us to the second point.

2. *Our "Givens" Do Not Originate with Us and Are Neither to Our Credit nor Our Blame*

The person who excels you in natural advantages has nothing whatever to justify his feeling superior. He had nothing to do with it. Is he handsome? He could have been born as ugly as Beethoven. Is he intelligent? He could have been retarded from birth. Is he physically strong? He could have been born crippled; for that matter he could be crippled yet through accident or illness beyond his control.

As the Scripture says, "Who makes you different from anyone else? What do you have that you did not receive? And if you did receive it, why do you boast as though you did not?" (1 Cor. 4:7). One has no reason to be proud of his "givens," and one has no reason to be ashamed of them. It is God's doing, not ours.

If you understand this "then you will not take pride in one man over against another" (1 Cor. 4:6). It follows then that you should not "take pride" in another over yourself; you should not feel inferior.

You shouldn't be blind to your weaknesses. That is hardly a sane self-evaluation. What you should do is decline to take as your responsibility what is God's work. Decline to take it as a personal discredit to you when others naturally excel you in some way, or even in many ways.

3. *Inferior Skills Do Not Make an Inferior Person*

If anyone can properly be identified as inferior, it is the person deficient in character, not in skills.

To understand this, consider the other side: the person with superior skills. Let's say a man is the world's best swimmer or chess player or test pilot. Would that make him a superior person even if he were selfish and dishonest and cruel?

He might think so, especially since the world would acclaim his accomplishments and heap praise on him. Actually, if he were of poor character, this inflating feedback from the world would only make him arrogant and thus more flawed than before. A graphic example of this is seen in Haman, whose case is examined in chapter three.

The good news in all this is that *you do not need to be inferior* because good character traits, which are true marks of your quality as a person, can be developed. As Scripture says, "Make every effort to add to your faith goodness; knowledge; self-control; perseverance; godliness; brotherly kindness, love" (2 Pet. 1:5-7).

Assuming that you do not have a poor character and no intention of acquiring one, we come to our fourth point.

4. *God Uses "Inferior" People as Much as Gifted People*

God cannot use everyone in the same way. He is not going to use a person with no musical ability to write great symphonies or move multitudes toward God with stirring renditions in song.

Nevertheless, God can and will wonderfully use the weakest and most helpless human beings. Robert H. Schuller gives the following example:

> I think of a husband and wife who have three healthy daughters and a young son who is a mongoloid. "We love all our children equally. But we *enjoy* our son the most," the father told me. "Perhaps it is because we know the others can get along on their own. But we know that he needs us. And we all need to be needed. When I come home from work, even though I have accomplished great things in my profession of engineering, I pick up my little boy with the slanted eyes and feel his thin arms curl around my neck. I hold him tight and in that supreme moment I know that I am a very important person to him. In that divine second I have an enormous and overwhelming sense of self-worth."[1]

Surely God was using that mongoloid child. Similarly, who has not seen or heard of God using a sick or lost child to touch the hearts of wayward parents or even of whole communities?

The Bible abounds with examples of God using the inferior.

> But God chose the foolish things of the world to shame the wise; God chose the weak things of the world to shame the strong. He chose the lowly things of this world and the despised things—and the things that are not—to nullify the

things that are, so that no man may boast before him (1 Cor. 1:27-29).

A LOAF OF BARLEY BREAD

I understand feelings of inferiority. I grew up in a home where I was the youngest of four children. My mom, dad, and all my siblings were older, bigger, smarter, and more powerful than me. They reminded me of this every time they called me Babe.

I felt like the typical raw recruit in the armed services, of whom it is said that they must salute everything that moves and paint everything that doesn't.

I dealt with self-doubt through withdrawal. I kept people at a distance. I figured what others didn't know about me and my business couldn't hurt me.

This attitude caused others to misunderstand me. I was seen as aloof, arrogant, or hostile, when I actually was unsure of myself. I wanted friends, I wanted people to like me, but at the same time, I practically shoved people away and warned them to keep their distance.

One particular experience symbolized my early life. It happened one winter during the austere early days of my Bible training. I was living with my little family in extremely humble quarters in a small town far from my ancestral home. We were very poor.

We couldn't afford garbage service. As wastes accumulated, I tried to bury them out in the yard. The ground was frozen rock-hard, however, so I couldn't bury anything very deep.

I was out there one day, scratching at the frozen earth and realizing I wasn't digging deep enough, when a town native passed by. He called a friendly greeting from the road and would have engaged me in conversation, but I was short with him. I didn't want him to know what I was doing.

As a result, I not only turned away a brother who wanted to be a friend, I also prevented myself from learning what he surely would have told me at once—that in their town municipal garbage service was provided without charge to all residents.

It has taken me a long time to overcome my self-doubt and inferiority feelings. The Bible has helped because in its pages I found many characters with whom I could identify. In fact, the noblest characters in the record were full of self-doubt. Joseph was the youngest in his family and despised by the others. David was the youngest, too, a nobody who was not even considered when the brothers were evaluated to see who might be Israel's future king. Moses told God he couldn't speak well enough to be the Lord's servant. Likewise Jeremiah said, "Ah, Sovereign Lord, I do not know how to speak; I am only a child" (Jer. 1:6).

Of all the biblical characters, none has helped me with my feelings of inferiority more than Gideon, whose story is told in Judges 6-8.

Gideon lived in a time when the land of Israel was devastated by a foreign invader, the Midianites. Whatever the Israelites produced in crops and herds was confiscated, and the people were reduced to living like fugitives in their own land.

To belong to a nation of oppressed people doesn't do a whole lot for one's positive self-image in the first place, for we all have a certain group identity.[2] Gideon comes along when being an Israelite is in some ways detrimental to his self-esteem. Besides that, he leads a furtive, demeaning life, trying to survive under the oppressive hand of a superior foreign power.

We see Gideon for the first time "threshing wheat in a winepress to keep it from the Midianites" (Judg. 6:11). Gideon cannot harvest any wheat in the open. He has to sneak a little of it into the winepress where he hopes he can thresh it without being detected.

"When the angel of the Lord appeared to Gideon, he said, 'The Lord is with you, mighty warrior'" (v. 12).

Do you get the irony of that greeting? "Mighty warrior"? "Timid pussycat" would better fit Gideon's actions and feelings at the time.

Then Gideon said to him, "But sir, if the Lord is with us, why has all this happened to us? Where are all his wonders that our

39

father told us about? But now the Lord has abandoned us" (v. 13).

Reading Gideon's responses is like reading a list of factors that damage self-esteem:

- "Why has this happened?" (I must be very bad to deserve this.)
- "Where are the wonders of our fathers?" (I don't measure up to my forebearers.)
- "The Lord has abandoned us." (I'm really angry at God, but that's blasphemous. Since I can't blame him, I have to blame me.)
- "But Lord, how can I save Israel? My clan is the weakest in Manasseh, and I am the least in my family" (v. 15).

More self-deprecating factors:

- "How can I save Israel?" (I can't do anything.)
- "My clan is the weakest." (I have no breeding.)
- "I am the least." (I get no respect.)

But the Lord said to him, "I will be with you, and you will strike down all the Midianites together" (v. 16).

We need to notice two important things about the selection of Gideon because they reflect how God can use us who feel inferior today.

First, God makes us more than we could be otherwise. The first words spoken to Gideon were, "The Lord is with you, mighty warrior" (v. 12). As we have already observed, that description did not at all fit Gideon as he was. However, it did fit Gideon as God intended him to become.

You may be keenly aware of your inadequacies. These weaknesses and failings may be very real, not just imagined. Gideon's experience demonstrates that, in the will of God, weaknesses can actually be turned into strengths.

Instead of bemoaning your inferiority, then, be sensitive to the voice of God calling you to become something better. People do change, you know. Perhaps certain formal training would help you. Maybe God himself will tutor you in the school of life. However it happens, remember that if God is calling you to a work, he will enable you to do it. "The one who calls you is faithful and he will do it" (1 Thess. 5:24).

Second, God can use us even with our limitations and inadequacies. In the midst of his protests of unfitness, Gideon heard the Lord say, "Go in the strength you have. Am I not sending you?" (Judg. 6:14).

In the glorious tradition of all great men of God, Gideon was to do exploits not because of his own might, but because the Lord was using him.

The Lord can use you too. It is true that God requires not so much our ability as our availability. He used an ordinary stick in the hand of Moses to part the waters of the Red Sea. He used an ass to rebuke the madness of Balaam the prophet. He used an obscure girl named Mary to give birth to his only begotten son, then cradled him in a humble cattle stall and announced the event not to heads of state but to shepherds.

Yes, and he used a once-frightened Gideon and a band of three hundred men to rout a Midianite army of one hundred thirty-five thousand soldiers.

God not only can use the inferior, he seems to delight in doing so. As he told Gideon concerning the army of thirty-two thousand men he had originally gathered, "You have too many men for me to deliver Midian into their hands. Israel may not boast against me that her own strength has saved her" (Judg. 7:2).

BARLEY-LOAF PEOPLE

Someone says, "I like what you are teaching, but I still feel so inferior."

Yes, and God understands your doubts and fears. He knows they don't go away overnight. Gideon required signs before he could surmount his doubts. Even after twice "putting out the fleece" and seeing God act on his behalf, Gideon needed assurance. But the point is that he was open and responding and following God one step at a time. That is what we must do.

For Gideon, the climax came the night before the battle was to begin. God sent his "mighty warrior" under a cover of darkness to spy out the enemy camp. Even here he accommodated Gideon saying, "If you are afraid to attack, go down to the camp with your servant Purah" (7:10). Evidently, Gideon was afraid because he did take Purah and go down.

At the edge of the enemy camp, the two spies overheard a conversation between some guards. One said, "I had a dream. A round loaf of barley bread came tumbling into the Midianite camp. It struck the tent with such force that the tent overturned and collapsed."

His friend answered, "This can be nothing other than the sword of Gideon. God has given the Midianites and the whole camp into his hands" (7:13,14).

As you can imagine, that was encouraging to Gideon. But don't miss the significance of the symbolism in the dream. Gideon was represented by a loaf of barley bread. Not by an armored chariot, suggesting grand military might, but by a humble product of the land. Furthermore, this loaf of bread that symbolized Gideon was not baked from wheat or rye or oats, but from barley.

Have you ever eaten barley bread? Probably not. We have a fancy new bakery in our community. I called to ask them about their varieties of bread. "We have about eighty to one hundred varieties of bread on any given day," they said. Did they have any barley bread? No.

I called a major milling company that distributes grains and flour to bakeries. They knew of no one who bakes barley bread, though some specialty breads do have a mixture of flours that includes some barley.

The reason barley bread is practically nonexistent is because it is so inferior!

Had Gideon seen himself as the humblest member of the least family in Manasseh? Was he a nobody? It was true. He wasn't from the finest of the wheat. He was coarse barley. God offered Gideon no illusions about himself to counter those marks of inferiority. He only showed that even a barley loaf, in the plan and purposes of God, could knock down and destroy the tents of Midian and bring deliverance to God's people.

God offers you no illusiions either. Perhaps a sane self-evaluation will reveal you as a person not rich in natural endowments. So admit that. Accept it. But remember too that God can do amazing things with barley-loaf people who are committed to him.

TIME TO CONSIDER

1. A country song facetiously laments, "O Lord, it's hard to be humble when you're perfect in every way." How do most "advantages" people have also carry their own disadvantages?

2. Is the idea that anyone is inferior strictly an illusion? Do you agree with my statement, "Some people generally are inferior to most others" (p. 35)? Why is it hard to talk people out of feeling inferior? Could it be because they know deep inside that they are?

3. How does 1 Corinthians 4:7 rule out both shame and pride over our basic abilities?

4. How are feelings of inferiority usually based on mixed-up values? In other words, what kinds of traits really do mark one as an inferior or superior person?

5. Does God want us to become better and more skilled so that he can use us, or does he want to use us as we are with all our weaknesses and limitations?

6. Feelings of inadequacy dogged many biblical characters such as Moses, Jeremiah, Gideon, and even Paul. Why didn't their inadequacy feelings keep them from serving God effectively?

4
. . .

The Pride Problem

"The Bible never has anything good to say about pride," the preacher thundered. "Pride is a word consistently used in a negative, evil sense."

I had heard it a hundred times before. I had preached it myself with all the conviction of "thus saith the Lord."

Did not the brilliant archangel Lucifer fall from heaven and turn into the devil because of pride? Did not Adam and Eve fall from innocence and plunge the human race into sin because, in pride, they wanted to be like God?

Even my "sane self-evaluation" text mentions first the danger of pride: "Do not think of yourself more highly than you ought" (Rom. 12:3).

Why, then, should I or any other Christian teacher seek to build people's self-esteem? Isn't self-esteen just another name for pride?

Clearly, some definitions are needed. In the New Testament,

three different Greek words relate to pride. The derivations of these words are interesting and highly instructive.

Huperephanos (proud) is formed by combining *huper* (above) with *phainomai* (to appear, be manifest) and literally means "to show oneself above others." Notice the strong element of comparison. Pride, by this definition, has nothing to do with self-esteem but with exalting yourself above someone else.

The second word, *tuphoo* (proud, high-minded) has its origin in *tuphos*, which means "smoke." The idea seems to be that as smoke obscures an object, so pride obscures the true nature of a person. Pride is pretense; it's putting on airs. As Romans 12:3 says, it is thinking of ourselves "more highly than we ought."

A third Greek word related to pride, though not so translated, is *phusioo*, which means "to puff up or inflate." Again it is the idea of falsehood, of appearing bigger than we are in reality.

Pride, then, is exalting oneself above others or assuming a self-congratulatory stance not justified by the facts. Self-esteem, by contrast, does not depend on comparison with others. It is based on truth not illusion.

Paul contrasts sinful pride with self-esteem when he writes, "If anyone thinks he is something when he is nothing, he deceives himself. Each one should test his own actions. Then he can take pride in himself, without comparing himself to somebody else" (Gal. 6:3,4).

The Greek term translated "take pride" is not one of the three expressions mentioned above, which are always used negatively. Here the original is *kauchema*, which means to glory or exult or boast. When the Lord approves "glorying" in our genuinely good traits or deeds, he is encouraging self-esteem.

To clothe these various definitions in flesh and blood, let's consider a classic biblical case of a proud and arrogant man. In the Bible, one character stands out as a supreme example of conceit: Haman. The account is in the book of Esther, one of the best stories ever written in terms of plot, characterization, and development.

We'll look at only a part of this magnificent story, namely

chapters 3-6. We will condense the story from the biblical text. As you read, try to analyze the character of Haman. What kind of person is he? What makes him behave as he does?

"After these events, King Xerxes honored Haman son of Hammedatha, the Agagite, elevating him and giving him a seat of honor higher than that of all the other nobles. All the royal officials at the king's gate knelt down and paid honor to Haman, for the king had commanded this concerning him. But Mordecai would not kneel down or pay him honor.

"When Haman saw that Mordecai would not kneel down or pay him honor, he was enraged. Yet having learned who Mordecai's people were, he scorned the idea of killing only Mordecai. Instead Haman looked for a way to destory all Mordecai's people, the Jews, throughout the whole kingdom of Xerxes" (Esther 3:1,2,5,6).

So Haman slandered the Jews and got the king to condemn them all to death. No one knew that Esther, the queen, was a Jew until after the unalterable edict went forth. Probably not knowing what to do but to trust God to work somehow, Esther got the principles together; the king, herself, and Haman for a banquet. She then scheduled a similar get-together for the next day.

"Haman went out that day happy and in high spirits. But when he saw Mordecai at the king's gate and observed that he neither rose nor showed fear in his presence, he was filled with rage against Mordecai. Nevertheless, Haman restrained himself and went home.

"Calling together his friends and Zeresh, his wife, Haman boasted to them about his vast wealth, his many sons, and all the ways the king had honored him and how he had elevated him above the other nobles and officials. 'And that's not all,' Haman added. 'I'm the only person Queen Esther invited to accompany the king to the banquet she gave. And she has invited me along with the king tomorrow. But all this gives me no satisfaction as long as I see that Jew Mordecai sitting at the king's gate.'

"His wife Zeresh and all his friends said to him, 'Have a gallows built, seventy-five feet high, and ask the king in the

47

morning to have Mordecai hanged on it. Then go with the king to the dinner and be happy.' This suggestion delighted Haman, and he had the gallows built.

"That night the king could not sleep; so he ordered the book of the chronicles, the record of his reign, to be brought in and read to him" (Esther 5:9-6:1).

Did the king think if anything would put him to sleep, it would be the history books? We don't know, but we clearly see the hand of God, who is not once mentioned in the entire book. It is on this particular night before Haman is to ask Mordecai's execution that the king can't sleep, and the particular part of the history the king reads describes how Mordecai once saved the kingdom by reporting a conspiracy.

" 'What honor and recognition has Mordecai received for this?' the king asked.

" 'Nothing has been done for him,' his attendants answered.

"The king said, 'Who is in the court?' Now Haman had just entered the outer court of the palace to speak to the king about hanging Mordecai on the gallows he had erected for him.

"His attendants answered, 'Haman is standing in the court.'

" 'Bring him in,' the king ordered.

"When Haman entered, the king asked him, 'What should be done for the man the king delights to honor?'

"Now Haman thought to himself, 'Who is there that the king would rather honor than me?'" (Esther 6:3-6).

Thinking it was for him, Haman cooked up the best rewards he could: to wear the king's robe and crown while being paraded through the city on the king's horse, escorted by one of the king's noblest princes, and proclaimed to everyone as "the man the king delights to honor" (Esther 6:9).

Imagine the shock, the crestfallen face, the leaden heart with which Haman heard the king's next words:

" 'Go at once,' the king commanded Haman. 'Get the robe and the horse and do just as you have suggested for Mordecai the Jew, who sits at the king's gate. Do not neglect anything you have recommended'" (Esther 6:10).

The story continues with other delightful twists and turns. We will not pursue it further, however, but will analyze the character of Haman. What can we observe about him from the record?

The most revealing insight into Haman's character comes from his own mouth. "I'm the only person Queen Esther invited to accompany the king to the banquet she gave" (Esther 5:12). There you have it, the dead giveaway. Haman's self-image hinges on comparing himself with others. Would it matter if someone else had attended the banquet too? Can't another receive equal recognition without it detracting from him?

Another could, if Haman's self-esteem were properly based on himself alone. But not if he is proud, not if he must show himself above others because his excellence is so much smoke, so much puff.

Another key to Haman's character is his intense concern over what people think of him. It is not self-interest that drives Haman so much as self-glorification. He already has everything a person might want, the highest position in the kingdom. Yet he says, "All this gives me no satisfaction as long as I see that Jew Mordecai sitting at the king's gate" (Esther 5:13).

We see his insatiable hunger for glorification again when he tells the king what honors should be heaped on his head.

This adulation compulsion reveals that Haman based his self-evaluation on the feedback he got from his world. Since that world praised him lavishly, he had an exaggerated opinion of himself. But when one man refused to defer to him, the entire structure on which his self-esteem rested was threatened. He determined to destroy a whole race of people to preserve his fragile self-esteem.

Interestingly, Haman was probably by nature an able and likable person. How else could he have achieved such striking success? After all, he was not born to prominence; he rose to it. But because he based his self-esteem on the world's feedback, a sane self-evaluation was impossible for Haman. What a tragedy!

The tragedy was by no means Haman's alone, however. He

might have been of great service to God and the people with his energy, ingenuity, and power. Instead the man became vicious, destructive, and nearly a murderer.

While you and I may never reach the same level of prominence as Haman, the principles observable in his life operate in us as well.

Who suffers if you or I lack a sane self-evaluation?

We do, but so does everyone else whose life we touch. We may become hateful and violent like Haman. Or the mischief may be much more subtle. Our disorder may betray itself only by a cutting remark about another person, or a remark that slips out without our realizing why.

Pride can also destroy Christian fellowship and damage the community of believers by producing in us a spirit of aloofness, as it did in Jennifer.

TWICE WRONG

Jennifer was caught in the double bind of pride and low self-esteem existing in the same person at the same time. She is outgoing by nature. Her thoughts and feelings surface easily. However, Jennifer found herself in a relationship in which her self-expression was often put down.

Actually, in the early stages of her relationship with her husband, Jennifer *was* wrong most of the time. She was young, naive, and barely out of her teens. She didn't know the Lord and had little training in the Scriptures.

Ben was a strong Christian and an active outdoor evangelist. He met Jennifer on the street, led her to the Lord, and eventually married her. He became not only her leader/teacher but her leader/husband.

As the years passed, however, and Jennifer grew to maturity as a Christian, the old way of relating that was established between them continued. Whatever she said or did that disagreed with Ben's views, he judged, condemned, or criticized. Jennifer felt enormous pressure to conform to whatever Ben wanted her to be, to think, to do.

Deferring to Ben as she did, Jennifer also developed a deferential attitude toward others whom she saw as her superiors. She assumed they, too, expected her to conform to their ideas of what she should do and be. So she played roles. Whatever the Superior People wanted her to do and be, she attempted. But trying to be what she thought each person wanted led to great confusion. Which role was really Jennifer?

As poor as her self-esteem was, however, Jennifer also had a pride problem. Ben had taught her the classical legalistic Christianity that governed his life: a list of narrowly prescribed dos and don'ts. Jennifer kept all the rules on the list quite well, and that became her badge of merit.

In her pride, Jennifer judged other people by whether or not they obeyed her list of rules. Most fell far short of her requirements. Jennifer could have no fellowship with such people because they were compromisers, unfaithful Christians. Since they obviously didn't mean business about living for Jesus, she couldn't waste much time on them.

Meanwhile, Jennifer revered those who were spiritual in her eyes. They were on a pedestal, and all she could do was try to be what they would approve. Consequently, Jennifer had no true fellowship with them, either. She was emotionally alone.

This went on for about nine years. A change began when the proud, rule-keeping Jennifer opened her heart just a wee bit to wonder if there might actually be some hidden sins in her own life. The Lord began to speak to her about the sins of the heart: bitterness, anger, jealousy, envy. And pride. When God showed her how proud she had been in her attitude toward Christians who were "beneath her," Jennifer was devastated. She literally cried and repented for a week.

When Jennifer repented of her pride, she no longer had that as a substitute for wholesome self-esteem. This enabled her, over the next two years, to see how much she lacked it.

The Lord had shown Jennifer how invalid and wrong it was for her to judge others. She had realized that the failings she thought she saw in them were not necessarily worse than failings she did not see in herself.

Slowly, she began to see that for anyone to have a judgmental, critical attitude toward her was just as wrong as for her to have such an attitude. Other Christians did not have to be what she thought they should be; they were accountable to God, not to her. By the same token, she didn't have to be what someone else, even Ben, thought she should be. She was accountable to God.

What glorious freedom this brought!

It meant she didn't have to role play any more. She didn't have to try to be what others thought she should be. She only had to be herself, in a humble walk with her heavenly Father.

Jennifer had escaped the hall of mirrors.

TIME TO CONSIDER

1. What distinctions can you make between pride and wholesome self-esteem? Which phrase in Romans 12:3 describes pride? Which phrase describes wholesome self-esteem? Which phrase in Galatians 6:3,4 describes pride? Which phrase describes wholesome self-esteem?

2. Can one be proud and have low self-esteem at the same time? Check this question against the phrases you identified in Galatians 6:3,4 (question one). Why do people with low self-esteem actually face increased temptation to be proud?

3. How do you affect others when you are proud? What are the effects when you have wholesome self-esteem?

4. Why and how are people with low self-esteem a threat and a danger to others?

5
...

What Is Your Name?

Little Sally told her mother at bedtime one evening that she had learned a new prayer in Sunday school. She wanted to say it instead of her usual "Now I lay me down to sleep." Her mother agreed but was surprised when Sally began, "Our Father who art in heaven, hello, what be thy name?"

God might well ask you a similar question: "My child reading this book, hello, what is your name?"

Of course, God already knows your name. However, the Lord does ask us questions when he already knows the answers. He asked Peter three times in succession, "Do you love me?" (see John 21:15-17). He asked not because he didn't know the answer, but because he wanted Peter to think about the issue the question raised.

God wants you to think about your name. Not so much the name on your driver's license or birth certificate, but the name by which you know yourself.

In the Bible, names mean something. God changed the names of quite a few people to better describe who he intended them to be. Abraham, Sarah, Israel, and Peter are known examples. Even Jesus was divinely assigned his name: "You are to give him the name Jesus (Savior), because he will save his people from their sins" (Matt. 1:21).

You bear several names that describe you. They serve as labels for your basic self-concept. You have:

- a name to describe your most basic nature
- a name to describe your present condition or state of mind
- a name to describe your relationship with God
- a name to describe your prospects for the future

In each of these areas God wants you to have a good name. If your present name is bad, he wants to change it. Even if your present name is good, he may want to change it to something better.

A NAME TO DESCRIBE YOUR MOST BASIC NATURE

Sinner! Sinner! Sinner! Many of us have sinned so much and been confronted with it so often we wear that name as our badge. We are stuck with it and don't realize God has changed our name to something much better.

Many hymn books include an old song entitled, "Only a Sinner Saved By Grace." It talks about the fact that we have not deserved God's favor; we have sinned against him. He accepts us totally through the merits of another, namely Jesus Christ our Lord.

However, the title of the song, which is also a recurring phrase in the chorus, is unfortunate. You and I are *not* only sinners saved by grace. We are much more than that. God did more than just forgive us when we trusted in Christ. He regenerated us. He made us new creatures and adopted us into his family. He came to indwell us in the person of the Holy Spirit. He united himself to us so that we could be one spirit with him. And he gave us the new name "Saint" to replace "Sinner."

54

Of course, we have had the name sinner for a reason. We earned it. I think of a woman who was more than forty years of age when she told me of her painful childhood. Even after so many years, her voice trembled with emotion as she talked. Her wound had been so deep and the pain so great that she had difficulty dealing with the memory.

"I was overweight as a girl," she said, "and my father had this terrible nickname for me. He called me Fats. How I hated it! He would come out on the front porch and call me in from play. 'Fats, come home!' I can still see myself sneaking in through the backyard lest anyone see me answering to that awful name."

Calling this girl Fats was bad on at least two counts, apart from how it wounded her feelings. First, it ignored everything else about her and focused on one undesirable trait as if that were her basic or entire nature. Second, it tended to perpetuate the negative trait by causing her to think of herself in those terms.

Just as that young woman had too much flesh on her bones, you and I have sin in our lives. We might even say that sin has been *characteristic* of us. But God has made us new creatures in Christ and has given us a *new* name.

Some Christians have difficulty believing that they should be called saint rather than sinner. It sounds strange to contemporary ears because the idea persists that a saint is some rare, super-holy Christian, probably one long dead, whom the church has proclaimed a saint.

However, the apostle Paul called all the Christians "saints" in his letters to the various churches of his time. Even the Corinthians, who were perhaps least holy in their behavior, were repeatedly called saints.

Saint, which means *holy*, is appropriate for all Christians for two reasons. First, the perfect holiness of Christ is put into our account when we receive Christ as Savior and Lord. God sees us in Christ as holy and without blemish.

Second, God intends us to become holy in character and practice. Saint is a name into which we grow. Sinner is a name we are to cast off as no longer descriptive of us.

Thus Paul mentions various sinner types—idolaters, thieves, sex perverts, slanderers—and then says, "And that is what some of you were. But you were washed, you were sanctified, you were justified in the name of the Lord Jesus Christ and in the Spirit of our God" (1 Cor. 6:11). Note that the passage says sinner is what you *were*, not what you are. In fact, Scripture teaches that our old sinful man is dead, crucified with Christ, and we are to count ourselves "dead to sin but alive to God in Christ Jesus" (Rom. 6:11).

We are to exchange our old self-image for a new one: sinner for saint. To go through life adding a propositional put down from the Bible—you are a sinner—to all the other put downs with which we must cope, is to let Satan use God's truth to his own ends. God wants us to acknowledge our sinfulness and then move on into the new life of the redeemed.

We will have more to say on this great theme in chapter ten. For now, let us simply observe that many Christians, tragically, have only worsened an already poor self-image by a distorted application of Christian truth. They have bought the proposition that they are worthless sinners and have gotten stuck there.

An experience I had in Bible institute illustrates the point. The teacher had asked us to write on the subject, "What did Jesus see of value in man?" He explained that he did not want us to say that there was nothing of value in man for Jesus to see.

When the papers came in, what do you suppose they said? Many (including mine) said that man is a totally depraved sinner with nothing in him that could possibly be of any value to God. We supported our staunch orthodoxy with Scripture: "There is no one righteous, not even one. . . . All have turned away, they have together become worthless" (Rom. 3:10,12). "For all have sinned and fall short of the glory of God" (Rom. 3:23).

We knew that man was a sinner. But we didn't understand that, as far as God was concerned, man was a sinner worth saving.

This may sound like a flat contradiction to the verse just quoted from Romans 3:12, which says of mankind "all have become *worthless.*" The original Greek for *worthless* literally means "not useful." This well describes fallen man—he is of no use to God, he is unprofitable, and in that sense, he is worthless.

But fallen man still has intrinsic worth or value to God, and God sent his son to die for our redemption. Once redeemed, we become saints, and as we learned in chapter two, we have now become God's rich and glorious inheritance.

You might be helped in accepting your new name of *Saint* by considering the fact that *Sinner* never was the real, most basic you. That may sound incorrect or even doctrinally false to you, but please consider:

> As a Christian, you are even less an intrinsic host to sin than you were as a child of Adam. You have been born again into the family of God. God's seed in you is holy and cannot sin. You are on your way to an eternal kingdom where "nothing impure will ever enter" (Revelation 21:27). You are going to feel at home there. Totally at home, as you have never been before. You will not long for the old ways or the old days. You will not secretly miss your sins, for you will know that they were never really a part of you. They do not belong.[1]

Replacing the old name Sinner with the divinely bestowed new name Saint is going to make a critical difference in the way you live out your faith.

Question: What do sinners do?

Answer: They sin.

As long as you wear the name Sinner, you are going to have a lot of trouble with sin, guaranteed. As a Saint you will find it more appropriate to live godly in Christ Jesus.

> David understood this principal centuries ago. He said something that reveals the beautiful insight people of ancient times had about being God's righteous people, not "sinners."

57

It was on the occasion when David cut off Saul's coattail but spared his life. David explained why he would not harm Saul even though Saul was trying to kill him. He said he was not going to do evil just because others did. "My hand will not touch you," he assured Saul.

Then David said something we all need to take to heart.

It was an "old saying" already in David's time: "From evildoers come evil deeds" (1 Sam. 24:13).

David didn't see himself as an evildoer, so it wasn't for him to do evil deeds.[2]

Receive it. God's new name for you is Saint.

A NAME TO DESCRIBE
YOUR PRESENT CONDITION

As a Christian your most basic name is Saint, not Sinner. You also have a name that describes your attitude, state of mind, or mentality as you face life day by day.

A good example of this is Naomi, whose story is told in the Book of Ruth. Naomi returned to the little town of Bethlehem after being ten years in the neighboring country of Moab. All her old friends and acquaintances gathered around her. "Naomi!" they said, "Is it really you?" (see Ruth 1:19).

Naomi had gone through a rough ten years in Moab. Her husband and both of her sons had died and she was depressed about her life. When her former neighbors called her Naomi, she said, "Don't call me Naomi; call me Mara."

You see, Naomi means "pleasant" and Mara means "bitter." Naomi said they should call her Bitter, not Pleasant, because "the Almighty has made my life very bitter. I went away full, but the Lord has brought me back empty. Why call me Naomi?" (Ruth 1:20,21).

So ended what could have been a happy welcome home. That's the last we read of friendly greetings. No wonder. Bitter people repel others, just when friends are what they need.

The Book of Ruth goes on to describe a dramatic change in Naomi's fortunes. Her daughter-in-law Ruth marries a good and prosperous citizen of Bethlehem. Naomi becomes nurse to their son, who turns out to be in the direct lineage of King David and later of Jesus Christ.

With our perspective, we know that the "bitter" experiences of Naomi's life did not justify her taking the name Mara. Later events made that clear.

In times of difficulty, like Naomi, we tend to let the circumstances shape our mentality and impose unbecoming names on us. We become Bitter or Despairing or Envious or Unbelieving. Many Christians become Angry, but unlike Naomi, they are not honest or in touch with their feelings enough to know their own name. Many also wear the name Guilty because of a losing struggle with the power of sin. Perhaps we answer to Inadequate because we are a barley-loaf person clinging to wheat expectations or pretensions.

One of the most common names of defeated Christians is Powerless. Paul lived by that name for a while. "I have the desire to do what is good, but I cannot carry it out. The evil I do not want to do—this I keep on doing. What a wretched man I am!" (Rom. 7:18,19, 24).

Later, Paul recognized that Powerless was not a name God wanted him to keep. He wrote, "For God did not give us a spirit of timidity, but a spirit of power, of love and of self-discipline" (2 Tim. 1:7).

If you are presently going by a name unbecoming your status as one of God's own, take hope. By faith, adopt a new and better name. Your difficulties are not forever. Life may have brought and may yet bring some bitter experiences your way, but they don't have to change your name from Pleasant to Bitter. That name isn't fit for someone like you who is in the lineage of David and Jesus.

A NAME TO DESCRIBE
YOUR RELATIONSHIP WITH GOD

Throughout this book, we have said that we need to get our self-concept from God. We must see ourselves in the true mirror of his Word rather than in the distorted mirrors of this world's feedback. We must get the sane self-evaluation God can give us.

One Scripture specifically talks about God calling us by a certain name. "How great is the love the Father has lavished on us, that we should be called. . . ."

Do you know what follows? Do you know what God calls us?

". . . that we should be called *children of God*" (1 John 3:1). The phrase that follows is enlightening, too. It tells why God calls us his children—because "that is what we are!"

Not only does the Scripture call us God's children, but the Holy Spirit says the same thing to us inwardly. "The Spirit himself testifies with our spirit that we are God's children" (Rom. 8:16). Jerry Cook comments on this verse:

> The verb "testifies" is in a continuous present tense in the original language. It means God is always saying that. If you are led of the Lord—if you hear what he is saying to you at any given moment—it will be a reaffirmation in some form that you really are his child. You are not necessarily what you think you are or what others say about you, but you are God's child.[3]

What an honor it is for us that God should bestow this name upon us! It says we are *of him,* just as children are commonly identified by receiving their father's name. In Scandinavian families, names end with "son" or "sen"; they are contractions from John's son or Ole's son or Peter's son to Johnson, Olson, Peterson. In Ireland a person may be said to come of Shea, of Malley, or of Rourke (O'Shea, O'Malley, O'Rourke). In the Bible, the prefix Ben or Bar was attached to names, as in Simon Barjona, meaning son of Jonah.

When by virtue of receiving Christ you are called God's child, this is not a name casually tossed your way. It is a name conferred on you by God himself in contrast to those names you were called previously, such as child of the devil, child of wrath, or child of hell. No wonder John exclaims that being called a child of God is an expression of lavish love on God's part.

What the name "child of God" can do for you is exemplified by the experience of James Mallory, author of *The Kink and I*. Dr. Mallory was a physician and an active church member before he came to know Christ as Savior. As a successful, respected man in the community, he wouldn't be expected to have any self-image problems, perhaps, but he did.

After his conversion, the new name "child of God" gripped him. "This new identity was very meaningful for me," he wrote, "because as a youngster I was always trying to compensate for being scrawny and red-headed. And now I was a son of God!"[4]

Inside the respected doctor had lived for many years a scrawny red-headed kid. Only when he received God's new name for him was Jim Mallory freed from the liabilities of his childhood.

Are you also carrying around demeaning names from your past? Replace them with the name God bestows upon you. The Word of God and the Spirit of God testify together: you are called child of God.

A NAME TO DESCRIBE
YOUR FUTURE PROSPECTS

The most prominent of our Lord's twelve apostles was a man we know as Peter. However, his mother and father never heard of Peter. They named their little boy Simon. The very first time Simon ever met Jesus, the Lord gave him a new name. " 'You are Simon son of John. You will be called Cephas' (which, when translated, is Peter)" (John 1:42).

Peter means stone or rock. For Jesus to give Simon that name was ironic if not laughable. If ever a man was not a rock, it was

Simon. Jesus might better have called him Sandy, for he was about as reliable as shifting sand.

The most notorious example of Peter's unreliability was when, at the crucifixion, Peter denied three times that he was Jesus' disciple. This came within hours after he had sworn he'd die with the Lord rather than ever deny him.

Clearly, Jesus did not confer the name Peter upon Simon in recognition of his rock-like character. It was not a name that Simon earned. It was a name to describe not what Simon was but what he would become.

The change did not occur overnight. It was three years after he got his new name that Simon denied the Lord and demonstrated he was no rock. *But he did become one.* After Pentecost, when he was filled with the Spirit, Peter stood like a rock before the enemies of the gospel. These were the same men who had recently condemned Jesus to be crucified, and they had power to put Peter to death as well. Peter boldly declared, "God has made this Jesus, whom you crucified, both Lord and Christ" (Acts 2:36).

Do you see how God works differently from this world? God does not give us a good name after we've earned it. That's how we get our bad names. We reveal some flaw and the world saddles us with a corresponding bad name. Like Fats. God's way is to give us a good name, not typical of what we are *now*, but of what he wants us to become, a name into which we'll grow.

Peter was that kind of name for Simon. *Saint* is that kind of name for us. The Lord may have other names he wants to give you to describe your future, names quite different from those that seem to fit you now.

You need to hear and accept and begin to grow toward your new name or names. That isn't easy when the name seems so much beyond what you know yourself to be. You can accept your new name, however, by an act of faith just as others have done before you.

Take Abraham. His name was originally Abram, meaning "High Father." That was not a bad name to begin with; fathers

62

were honored in the patriarchal society of that day.

The trouble was that Abraham had great difficulty in living up to his name. His struggle to have a child forms the backdrop for the epic story unfolded in Genesis 12-21, a story spanning some twenty-five years of Abram's life. It is a story of repeated frustration as childless Abram continually fell short of the meaning of his name.

At last, when Abram was eighty-six years old, Ishmael was born to him and Hagar, his wife's servant. So Abram did become a father, but there was nothing particularly noble or high about it, and "High Father" still seemed quite beyond him.

At this point, when Abram hadn't fully attained the implications of his original name, God changed his name to Abraham, meaning "Father of a Multitude." God said he would become such a father not through Ishmael, but through a son yet to be born to Sarah his wife. This possibility seemed so remote to Abraham that he "fell facedown" and "laughed" (Gen. 17:17).

That's the way God's new names are. He sees more in us than our parents do. He sees more in us than the people around us do. He sees more in us than we do. So much more that when we hear his name for us, we too may be tempted to laugh.

But Abraham quit laughing when he realized it was up to him to choose whether or not he was going to believe this message. The most critical choice of Abraham's long and eventful life faced him at that moment, for his very soul's salvation depended on it.

What does the Bible say about Abraham's choice?

First, he openly faced the facts of his case. Abraham didn't just say, "OK, God, swell, I believe that I will be Father of a Multitude through Sarah." An easy statement such as that, devoid of any wrestling with the implications and difficulties, would also have been devoid of reality. You see, faith is not superficial. It's facing the issues honestly and still choosing to believe deeply.

Concerning Abraham, we read, "He faced the fact that his own body was as good as dead—since he was about a hundred

63

years old—and that Sarah's womb was also dead" (Rom. 4:19). These facts made Abraham laugh when he first heard his new name.

However, a new fact now entered the picture. God had said, "Your name will be Abraham, for *I have made you* a father of many nations" (Gen. 17:5, italics added).

Abraham's choice, after facing the facts, was either to believe what God said or to believe what he and everyone else "knew," that he and Sarah were unable to have children, period.

Your choice is similar. You will believe what you and others "always knew" about your being an inferior person, or you will believe something better about yourself because God says it.

The reason Abraham and you can believe the "something better" is not only that God says it. The reason is that the God who says it is also the Creator, and he can make it come to pass, regardless of your apparent natural potential. We are not talking here about simple positive thinking. All the positive thinking in the world could not make a one-hundred-year-old man sexually potent and his sterile and aged wife fertile. But God could.

That is what Abraham believed. He believed in a God who "calls things that are not as though they were" (Rom. 4:17). That faith, we read, was "credited to him as righteousness" (Rom. 4:22). In other words, his soul's salvation depended on it, as we indicated a bit earlier.

Ultimately, in full implementation of the promise, Abraham did become father of a multitude. Furthermore, and here's the point we must not miss, although the promise took a long time to materialize fully, Abraham got most of its benefits then and there. He saw himself in a completely different light. Instead of the barely-a-father-by-questionable-means image of himself that had controlled him, he now saw himself as what God said he would become: Abraham, father of many nations.

Do I have to say that Abraham lived as a happier and better man with his new self-image? Even his wife's name was changed at that time, and Sarai (Contentious) became Sarah (Princess). The Father of a Multitude and his Princess may have lived in the same old tent for a while, but it was a noble dwelling to them for they were noble people.

A NEW NAME FOR THE SUCCESSFUL PERSON

What God did for Abraham in replacing an old, deficient self-concept with a new and glorious name, he also did for others who chose to believe him.

Jacob was a pretty rotten guy, full of cute little tricks for taking advantage of people. Usually they worked, if getting what you want and not caring how you get it can be called working.

But how does a guy like that feel about himself? Oh, he may justify what he does. He may cover up. But deep inside, he can't like himself very much, can he?

Then, too, a person's devious behavior has a way of catching up. After all, people don't appreciate shabby treatment. Some have even been known to retaliate. Perhaps the worst part is that a Jacob never knows for sure what the people he has misused may be thinking. Thus, even after twenty years absence from home, Jacob feared that his brother Esau, whom he had cheated, might still be laying for him, looking to get even.

With all this garbage from his past life bugging him, Jacob had a memorable encounter one night with the Lord. There he received a new name, Israel. Jacob's new name meant "God's fighter," or "One who has power with God."

The point of all this is that even "successful" people have needs. You may not be a helpless, self-pitying clod. In fact, you may despise such weak people and see yourself as a resourceful, make-things-happen person who can take care of yourself. You are a fighter, a person of power. But are you God's fighter? Do you have any power with God?

If you are nowhere with God, your very strengths may lead you into disaster. Like Jacob, you may have habits and personality traits that make you successful but deep down also make you feel rotten about yourself. What about the people you associated with along the way? How did you treat them? How about your loved ones? What do they think of your priorities? How about your enemies? What could they say truthfully to your shame?

It's not that God necessarily wants to take the fight out of you. He may just want to change your name from "Dirty Fighter" to "God's Fighter." In any case, God has a name for you, and it's a good one. You need to plug it into your mental computer in place of all the bad names you've picked up along the way.

TIME TO CONSIDER

1. According to Proverbs 22:1, how important is it to have a good name? Do you think this "good name" refers to your legal name, your reputation, or your personal identity? How would you rank the three in order of importance?

2. Do you agree that God wants to change the name of every believer from Sinner to Saint? Why or why not? Have you undergone such a name change personally? Explain.

3. Adverse circumstances sometimes hang bad names on us such as Bitter or Angry or Depressed. Why is it a mistake to allow this, and how can we prevent or remedy it?

4. How can the name Child of God rescue us from feeling insignificant or worthless?

5. Which comes first in the ways of God with his people—the name or the nature? In other words, does God call us what we have become, or do we become what God has called us?

6. How can we accept a new name from God that does not fit us as we know ourselves to be?

7. Based on your insights from this study so far, what changes do you see in your life? What changes do you expect to see in the future?

Part II
How and Why People Degrade Others

6

...

Parents: They Bring You Up and Put You Down

Our daughter Krystal, her husband Bill, and their three girls moved into a new neighborhood. I hesitate to call Bill and Krystal ideal parents, but they come about as close as any I know. They are sensitive and loving, yet firm. They are keenly aware of the need to nurture their children's sense of worth.

Imagine Krystal's dismay, then, upon meeting a new neighbor, to hear her introduce her two-year-old son as Matt-brat.

Obviously, this mother was not aware of the damaging effect a demeaning name can have on a child. Tacking unflattering nicknames on children is only one way parents, who are supposed to bring their children up, often put them down. Another, and perhaps more common parental put down, is the negative put down characterizing remark.

Dr. Honor Whitney of Texas Women's University surveyed thousands of men and women to discover how many remembered hearing certain put down phrases from their parents.[1]

Nine of every ten surveyed remembered hearing, "How many times do I have to tell you?"

Other common phrases that make children feel bad include:
• Do you expect me to believe that?
• Look at you—you're a mess.
• When are you going to grow up?
• Can't you do anything right?
• That was a stupid thing to do.
• I guess I just can't trust you.
• You are a bad boy (girl).

A slightly different type of parental put down is the prophecy of failure:
• You'll never amount to anything.
• I pity you when you leave home.
• How do you ever hope to support a family?
• You'll never land a husband.

There is also the unfavorable comparison put down. "Look at this report card. You got a D in English again? Why can't you be like your brother Philip? He never gets below a B in anything."

When there is no brother or sister with whom to compare a child, parents may cite their own example. "Why is it so hard to get you to do anything around the house? I always *wanted* to help my mother; she had to work so hard cleaning up after the whole family."

So it goes. One way or another, parents often injure the self-esteem of their children.

Most parents, thank God, also build up their children in countless small but significant ways. They love their children and express that love by playing with them, praising their accomplishments, soothing their hurts, and listening to their childish prattle. Every such act on the part of a parent says, "You are important."

Think of the child, though, whose parents put him down constantly but never counter it by treating him with love and acceptance. The small child's whole world is his home. If the feedback there is all demeaning, the child has little chance of emerging unscathed.

The emotional damage inflicted on such a child is frightening, as the following true account by a young woman graphically reveals:

"Why?" The question hung in the air as my ten-year-old brother shifted his weight from one foot to the other.

"Robby," Mother repeated, "why did you cause so much trouble at school again?"

"I don't know," he muttered. "I . . . I'm sorry."

"Well, I don't know either," Mother said. "I just don't understand you. I wish you'd show some appreciation for all I do. What does it take to satisfy you? Maybe we should send you to a reform school."

She went on and on, reviewing everything Robby had done wrong in his entire short life.

I could hear it all from my room, and I knew how Robby felt. I felt the same way. In this home so lacking in physical expressions of love, we two had drawn closer together than most brothers and sisters. We confided in each other, built up torn egos, and mended tattered feelings. We loved and protected each other from our formidable parent.

That we should fear and hate our own mother had never seemed strange to us. We grew up hating her. We were, in her words, "worthless, useless, clumsy, and unappreciative." We could do nothing right. We became excessively shy and unsure of ourselves. I chewed my fingernails until they bled and became infected. Robby became rebellious.

"Go to your room and stay there until supper!" I heard her shout at him at last.

Robby shut himself in his room. As soon as I could, I joined him.

"Go away," he said.

I tried to help. "It doesn't matter what she says, Rob. You're not that bad."

"Yes I am," he said. "She's right. I'm no good. I can't do anything right. I shouldn't even be living." A strange, frightening

71

emptiness filled his eyes. His voice sounded drained of emotion.

"Leave me alone," he said in a whisper.

Hurt and confused, I left him. I walked outdoors, through a wooded area behind our house. I had often walked out here when depressed. I would look at the sky and talk to God. I wanted to know him and feel his love.

We needed love so much. Mother was so impatient and exacting; she never smiled at us or hugged us. Dad was away so much on business that he didn't realize what was happening.

"God, you must care," I cried. "You've just got to." I stayed until Mother called.

I started back to the house. In the middle of the woods, a rustling in the trees caught my attention. I looked up and saw legs dangling through the leaves. My heart froze.

"Robby!" I screamed. I tore through the brush and climbed the tree. The branches and vines fought me, scratching at my face and arms. My fingernails began to bleed from my struggle with the heavy rope. It was thick, and the knot held, tightened by the weight of Robby's swaying body. Sweat ran down my forehead and stung my eyes.

"O God," I prayed, "if you care about us at all, help me. Please!"

Robby was no longer moving. I remembered the small jack-knife he carried in his pocket. I searched, grasped it, and cut at the rope. Robby flopped to the ground. I scrambled down and cradled his head in my hands.

"Robby, Robby, please be all right!" I sobbed over and over. "You can't give up. God loves us. I know it. He helped me save you." I looked down at his face and through blurry eyes saw him smile weakly at me.

"Do you really think so?" he asked, his voice raspy.

"Yes," I said. "He gave you another chance. Maybe we can get to know more about God. We could start going to that Sunday school on the hill."

"Mom will never take us," he said, crying.

"We can walk. It's not far."

With the help of some wonderful Sunday school teachers, we

gained self-confidence. Our home life didn't change overnight. But God had begun to work. He never let up.[2]

Robby's story, no thanks to his parents, had a happy ending though his scars no doubt remain. How much different and better Robby's life might have been had his parents contributed to his sense of worth from the beginning.

As Jane Merchant's parents did.

Jane was born with *osteogenesis imperfecta*, a congenital bone disease causing the bones to fracture easily. Jane never walked, became bedridden at age thirteen, and lived as a "helpless invalid" for the next forty years until her death in 1972. She was deaf for the last thirty years of her life.

Not surprisingly, Jane struggled with her own sense of worth, but she came through in grand style. Her two-thousand poems blessed the lives of many, and though she never attended school, one of her fans, a professor at the University of Tennessee, spoke of her as the best educated person he had ever encountered.

God's earliest provision for developing Jane's sense of worth was unusually wise and loving parents. They treated her consistently as a useful and unique member of the household. Thus, despite her own limitations and the low estate of her parents, who lost their farm to drought and the depression and lived on the edge of poverty most of their lives, Jane Merchant had a profound sense of her own worth.

She knew the importance of self-respect and the deadliness of self-pity. She wrote of both in her poem "Purchase," which tells of a young man who, like her, was deaf.

I almost bought a dozen combs today,
A dozen combs I didn't need at all,
Because the thin boy offering the array,
At the back door, of various large and small
Combs of all kinds and colors, when I said,
"Good Morning," showed me, with a resolute
White face, a narrow card on which I read

73

The neatly lettered words, "I'm deaf and mute."
A thrush was singing then. I would have bought
His whole supply, but that his look forbade
My charity; so after careful thought
I took just one, the finest one he had.
I could not sleep tonight if I had tried
To buy his courage of him, and his pride.[3]

Jesus said we must take heed to the little ones for they have a special place in the heart of the Father (see Matthew 18:1-10). Part of our responsibility is that we build up, not destroy, their sense of value as human beings. God says they *are special*, and woe to us if we convince them they are not.

TIME TO CONSIDER

1. Did the parental put down phrases (p. 70) bring back any painful memories from your childhood? If as many as ninety percent of those surveyed remembered some of the phrases, does it mean that nine out of ten children are abused? Do you think tone of voice is important as well as words spoken? Explain.

2. If you suffered verbal abuse as a child, do you find yourself treating your children as you were treated? If not, what do you think accounts for the difference? If so, what are you doing to change?

3. What's wrong with the way this mother communicates with her daughter: "Look at this cabinet! Water all over it. How many times do I have to tell you how to wash dishes? Can't you do anything right?" How would you suggest this mother deal with the situation?

4. Which of your actions and words build self-esteem in your child(ren)? How would you distinguish between build up and

puff up? Should you praise a child for being cute or pretty; kind or honest?

5. How does the example of Robby (p. 71) offer hope even for the severely abused child? How does the example of Jane (p. 73) offer hope for physically and materially disadvantaged children?

7
...

Put Downs, Put Downs, Everywhere Put Downs

A child fortunate enough to have sensitive, loving parents who never put him down is truly blessed. Even so, he will not venture far beyond the circle of his immediate family before he is put down by other people.

The put down may be very blunt. "Go away; we don't like you." Or it may be subtle but still unmistakably real and cruel.

Certainly when a youngster reaches school age, if not before, he will be victimized by that cruel childhood practice of choosing up sides. You know how it works. The gang is going to play ball and teams must be organized. Captains are designated, often by popular agreement. Then the captains set in motion a procedure that can only end in the humiliation of some of the children.

The captains choose players in order of (1) how well they think you can play the game, (2) how well they happen to like you.

If you can't play the game well, and if you are not particularly liked, you are in trouble. If you happen to be the least "choosable" of all, you are in big trouble. You are going to be put down openly, before everyone else in the group. It's almost as if you are on display, and the word is announced, "Look, everybody, this person is the least among us, the bottom of the heap, worthless."

Being shamed by one's peers can be an agonizing experience. But for some children, especially younger ones, it's even worse to be put down by an authority figure such as a teacher. This can be terribly damaging, and it's also rather common.

Levauna Smith, my sister, tells how she was turned off to school and wounded emotionally by an insensitive teacher. She was in fourth grade when the teacher walked the aisles one day observing the children coloring pictures. When she reached Levauna's desk, she asked critically, "Where did you ever learn to color sky?"

Levauna took the question quite literally. "At Kenwood," she replied, naming the school she had attended the year before. The whole class laughed, and Levauna gathered that she was not only stupid for answering as she had, but for coloring sky badly, though she never did know what was wrong—she used blue.

Later, the same teacher ridiculed her for saying that Old Ironsides was called that because it was an iron ship. Again the teacher and the other students laughed at her. If the teacher ever told her what was wrong with her answer, Levauna didn't hear it. She was too embarrassed and humiliated.

From then on, though she had been a good student, Levauna withdrew into a shell. She never volunteered an answer, and if the teacher asked her a question, she simply said she didn't know. She failed the fourth grade and never did well in school again.

The teacher had destroyed her self-esteem, had made her feel "dumb and ugly and worthless," and had so marred her life that it took her twenty years to get over it.

Most people could tell of similar experiences, though perhaps not so damaging. I certainly can recall a few unpleasant incidents from my own school days.

One that stands out occurred when I was in fifth grade. I was supposed to carry a placard in a school program. From center stage, I was to slip out between the heavy curtains at just the right time. At rehearsal, I failed to appear on cue once or twice because I couldn't see where the curtains parted. I told the teacher, but she didn't seem to believe me. "Stand right here," she told me impatiently, as she positioned me directly behind the center of the curtain.

I stood there, listening intently for my cue. I wanted so badly to do what I was supposed to and not make Mrs. Green angry. When I knew it was time, I attacked the curtain, hoping the invisible opening would indeed be there. It was—but the heavy material caught both sides of my placard, and I couldn't get through.

Mrs. Green was on me at once. "What happened *this* time?" she demanded.

"I couldn't get through," I replied. "My card's too wide."

"Well, of course you can't just shove it through straight ahead," she said, as if I were the dumbest person she had ever seen. She took the placard from my hands. "You have to turn it sideways and slip it through," she said. "Like this."

She could have done worse, I suppose. She could have taken the assignment away from me and given it to another child who would make it look easy. But the disdainful manner in which she corrected me made the effect almost as bad as if she had rejected me completely.

Later that year, I ran afoul with my art teacher. She told everyone in my class to cut out a picture of a ship from a calendar or magazine and bring it to school. "Don't tell me you can't find one," she said. "I'm sure you can if you look."

We had no magazines at our house and no calendars with a picture of a ship. Since the teacher had said she wouldn't accept excuses, I saw no choice but to fail the assignment.

When I showed up minus a ship, the teacher was upset.

79

"That's why you Baldwin kids always fail," she stormed at me in front of the whole class. "You just don't try."

That was too much. I took considerable pride in my good report cards, and I didn't care to be lumped in with others in the family who supposedly did not. I had to challenge her statement. "I never got a failing grade in my life!" I protested.

"Well, you *will* next report period," she said.

Sure enough, my next report card showed a failing grade in art. My homeroom teacher was Mrs. Rubeneck, and you can guess what the kids called her. "Mrs. Rubberneck" had a reputation for being tough, but we always got along fine. When she saw my grade in art, she asked what had happened. I told her, "The art teacher has it in for me."

"Oh no, I'm sure that's not true," Mrs. Rubeneck said. "I'll have a talk with her."

Through Mrs. Rubeneck's good offices, the art teacher learned I was not a negligent student. Her attitude toward me changed entirely and my art grade bounced right back up.

I had dodged the bullet. "Stupid" was not to become one of the bad names I would later have to shed.

GROWN UPS GET PUT DOWN TOO

Even when they leave childhood, people continue to receive the message in countless ways:
- you are not important
- you are not acceptable
- you are not desirable
- you do not measure up

Maybe we are not invited when others get together for a party or activity. Maybe our opinions are not sought when an issue is being discussed. If we volunteer our views, we may be ignored.

Some put downs are extremely subtle and quite unintentional. I cringed inside when I heard a pastor pray for a couple of teenage boys who had responded to his invitation to step forward after his sermon to receive salvation. He prayed that God would bless "Bob and his friend" as they made this important decision.

Bob and *his friend*? Even before God was this young man with Bob nobody in his own right? Did he only count as a friend of somebody else? Somebody named Bob who was important enough to be recognized?

I'm sure the pastor didn't mean to slight the young man. Apparently, he did not know his name. Maybe the young man didn't even notice. Still, it was a put down, however subtle and unintentioned. Along with a multitude of other personal put downs, it might have added its small weight of self-reproach.

Put downs come in many forms. We spoke in the previous chapter about *parental* put downs. Before that, in the chapter on our new names, we talked about *propositional* put downs—using theological propositions about the sinfulness of man to unduly beat down believers who should have moved from a sinner identity to that of a saint.

So far in this chapter, we've described *peer* put downs among children, *patronistic* put downs by teachers, and *personal* put downs that can come to us at any age and from anyone. We need now to give particular attention to what we will call *possessional* and *positional* put downs.

POSSESSIONAL PUT DOWNS

Our possessions can cause us self-esteem problems. I'm not talking about not being able to wear such nice clothes as others, not being able to drive such a fine car, or not living in so lavish a house—though these possessional shortfalls can damage self-esteem.

Even if you live on a par with those around you, your possessions can still cause you serious trouble. Every time anyone puts down something you own, your self-esteem comes under assault. The fact that you possess an item suggests you want it or find it acceptable. If someone else puts it down, he is saying something is wrong with you. Your judgment or your taste or your ability to provide for yourself is not very good. A more subtle message is that you are inferior to the one who is criticizing you.

The practice of putting down other people's possessions is a bad one. Unfortunately, some people do it constantly.

I knew a woman like that once. Whatever we had, she put it down. When we got a piece of furniture, she said it was "nice, but I wouldn't want it because that fabric tends to frizz and the store where you bought it sells inferior merchandise." If we got a new car, it was wonderful, but she wouldn't want it because those vinyl seats are so hot in the summertime. Besides, she knew so and so who had one like it and had nothing but trouble.

Why are we often inclined to behave like that woman? Why do we have to add our little "but" phrases when we say something nice? It has been observed that any time we make a "but" statement, the "but" cancels everything that went before it so far as the emotional impact on the other person is concerned. The "nice" comment is nullified, and the "but" remark is all that remains.

Suppose I said to you, "Friend, you are nice looking, but you are not wearing your hair right for the shape of your face." What would you carry away from that encounter? Would you go away feeling good and saying to yourself, "He thinks I am nice looking"?

Hardly. You would go away thinking, *Ohhhh, he doesn't like my hairstyle. It must be really bad.*

It's important to understand what's going on behind the scenes in a situation like this. Such understanding may help us stop injuring other people as well as spare us unnecessary injury at their hands.

To explain the dynamics of such an exchange between people, let me tell you about my brother's car purchase some time ago. "I got this great deal on a Chrysler," Ron told me. "Only cost me eight hundred dollars, and it's in wonderful shape. You've got to see it."

The first thing I noticed about the Chrysler was that the left front fender was a slightly different shade of green than the rest of the car. That meant one thing. The car had been in an accident, and the left front fender had been repainted.

My inclination was to point this out to Ron, to say something like, "It's really nice, *but* it has been in an accident."

I resisted the temptation. Instead I commented honestly on how beautiful the interior was, how good the general condition of the car seemed, and that it was a good buy.

If I had mentioned the fender, what would have been my reason? I mean, he had already bought the car. Beneath the surface I would have been saying, "Hey, I'm a very wise and observant person. I noticed something right away that you overlooked. I not only noticed it, I know what it means. What's the matter with you, dummy?"

The bottom line of such communication is "I'm smart and you are not."

The probable reason I would say such a thing is that I have difficulty with my own self-image. As a result, I need to extract some good feelings about myself whenever and however I can. So I do it at his expense.

Why can't we just give a gift? Why can't we just say it's nice, period? The inability to do so is a dead giveaway that we are not whole.

Jesus said, "Freely you have received, freely give" (Matt. 10:8). When we have received the emotional wholeness Jesus wants to give us, we will be able to give freely to other people with no "buts" attached.

I'm sometimes asked, "But what if a negative statement needs to be made? Suppose instead of the mismatched paint, you had discovered the brakes were faulty. What then? Would you still just say nice things so the other person would feel good?"

No. The error on one side is to put people down because we have problems of our own. The error on the other side is to be dishonest or even destructive in the name of being nice.

If I notice the brake pedal very slowly gives under continued foot pressure, I still don't have to say, "It's nice, *but.* . . ." I can say, "It's nice, *and* even though I think there may be a small problem with the brakes, that is a relatively minor expense, especially considering the great buy you made."

POSITIONAL PUT DOWNS

Closely related to the possessional put down is the positional put down. Just as your possessions represent you, so do your positions on political and religious matters. To some degree, your position on any issue is an extension of you.

When people put down your position, they detract from you as a person. It is appropriate to differ on issues without attacking the other person. Often, however, people put down the view that conflicts with their own as if it were ridiculous and no right-thinking person could possibly hold it. The one being subjected to this treatment senses, correctly, that he is being put down.

Dr. James D. Mallory, Jr. gives an example of this kind of interaction in his book *The Kink and I*:

> I got caught up in this one time in a conversation at a Christian Medical Society meeting. Two visiting freshmen began to reel off a lot of the statements that you will hear sometimes about Christianity being myth and about how man has learned all these new things that pretty well explode the outmoded concepts of the Bible. My reaction to these men was not exactly compassionate. They were coming across as confident in their "new" knowledge that was supposed to show us Christians we were all wrong.
>
> My ego response was, *Who do these two think they are? I worked through all that intellectual ego-trip years ago. I know better than that. They act as if they've got something new to tell me.* My ego was being threatened; they were implying I was not as smart as they. So I began to put them down, to point out that their line of thinking wasn't all that logical.

I had a flash of insight in the midst of this encounter that I was winning this battle but losing these two young men. It was an agonizing thing to realize that my witness was really an expression of my hostility. I was rejecting these fellows and puffing up my own ego.[1]

Dr. Mallory realized he was putting down these two young men, not just differing with them. The fact is, though, they had put him down first by the manner in which they spoke about Christian faith.

When you have everyone fighting for his own self-respect like that, no learning is likely to take place. Positions are hardened and hostilities entrenched. By contrast, when our faith is genuinely strong and we are emotionally whole, we are not easily threatened or disturbed by others' expressions of unbelief, and we can then witness to them effectively. We may even learn a few things in the process.

We have discussed various put downs for two reasons. First, you need to recognize what has gone into the formation of your personal self-image. If you have suffered from low self-esteem, you should better understand now why that has been so.

The second reason we've gone on at some length about put downs is that you need to realize the unintentional damage you can do to others. There is no assurance that knowing will help you do better. Those who put down others usually do so because of unsatisfied needs in their own lives. Simply reading a damage assessment is not likely to change their behavior because it leaves the needs unsatisfied.

Still, if you are a Christian, the knowledge that you are injuring others certainly ought to add urgency to your desire to get a true view of you. You will go on suffering and injuring others until you do.

The good news is that help for low self-esteem is not hard to find. It may be hard to appropriate though, because it requires you learn new ways of thinking. Replacing bad habits with good ones takes time, and that applies to mental habits as much as any others. That's all the more reason to begin in earnest right now.

Memorize some of the great biblical texts that reveal how you ought to view yourself: 1 Corinthians 4:7; Genesis 1:27; Psalm 8:4,5; Luke 12:6,7; Jeremiah 29:11; Psalm 139:14; 1 John 3:1; Isaiah 41:10.

Select a verse from this list that is particularly helpful to you. Memorize it, claim it, live by it. Make it your verse. Or appropriate them all. Yes, it will take some effort, but your self-esteem is at stake here. You need to be transformed by a renewed mind, a reprogrammed mind, a mind that thinks God's thoughts. That won't happen all by itself, but *it can happen*.

Will it happen to you?

TIME TO CONSIDER

1. This chapter identifies seven different sources of demeaning put downs. After each source listed below, place a number from one to ten indicating how much you have been put down (one is slightly affected; ten is severely damaged):

propositional (church
  teaching) _____

peer (other children) ____

personal (adult) _____

positional _____

parental_____

patronistic (teachers
  and leaders) _____

possessional _____

2. Within the past week, which kinds of put downs have you experienced or consciously resisted, either on the giving or receiving end? Which have you observed as a bystander?

3. What activities or people have you deliberately avoided because you didn't want to experience the put down you expected would be involved?

4. Do you sometimes check yourself from putting down another, as I did concerning my brother's car? If not, do you think it is because you have no inclination to put others down or

because you are not sufficiently sensitive and aware in this area to recognize it when it occurs?

5. Why is it not enough simply to understand the damaging effects of put downs? What more do you need in order to avoid putting down other people? How can you get this something more?

Part III
Failure Isn't Fatal–Necessarily

8

...

Sin: Failing
the Lord

Two major causes of low self-esteem combine to harass most people. One is from *without* and consists of put downs, as described in the previous chapter. The second major cause of low self-esteem is from *within* and consists of failures of various kinds. We tend to view our failures as clear and unmistakable evidence that we are not all we ought to be. Nobody else has to put us down or treat us shabbily. Our own hearts condemn us. The one kind of failure that makes us feel worst about ourselves as Christians is when we *sin*.

A poignant line from Jesus' story of the prodigal son says it well: "I have sinned against heaven and against you. I am no longer worthy to be called your son" (Luke 15:21). With the young man's feelings of guilt came also a deep sense of unworthiness.

We must not overlook the fact that this sense of unworthiness was not so great that it kept the young man from turning to his father. Neither was it a feeling that the father tried to perpetuate. The father restored the son to the full privileges of sonship with no further recrimination.

Our point here, however, is that guilt carries with it a sense of shame and damages self-esteem.

SECRET SINS

The story is told of a small western town that suddenly experienced a mass exodus of some of its leading citizens. Practically overnight, several families packed up their belongings and moved away.

It was all very mysterious, and then the truth came out. A prankster had sent identical anonymous letters all over town. The letters said, "The jig is up. By week's end, everyone will know exactly what you have done."[1]

Apparently, a lot of people had reason to fear that prospect, and they left town.

I ask you, though, what really changed as a result of those letters? Certainly the guilt or innocence of the recipients did not change. The letters only caused those who had done something shameful to become acutely aware of it and to contemplate the effect of exposure. This moved them to drastic action.

Let's get the clear picture.

The citizens in our little story were comfortably interacting with each other day by day. They held their heads high, looked one another in the eye, treated one another as equals—until the exposé threatened. In other words, they had good self-esteem. Then everything changed. They slinked out of town under cover of night, ashamed to show their faces.

Exposure or the imminent threat of exposure was what upset the people in our story. Yet, their hidden sin surely hurt their self-respect before that. It's likely that many times some chance encounter, some passing remark, some sight or sound or smell reminded them of their guilty secret and raised the fear that it might someday become known.

Secret sin in our lives is like termites in a house. Everything looks fine, but all the time the structure is being weakened and undermined. If nothing is done, it will ultimately collapse.

Secret sin undermines self-esteem, and it also has a way of becoming known sooner or later. Sin is hard to keep hidden. Jesus said, "There is nothing concealed that will not be disclosed, or hidden that will not be made known. What you have said in the dark will be heard in the daylight, and what you have whispered in the ear in the inner rooms will be proclaimed from the roofs" (Luke 12:2,3).

What can one do about secret sins and their insidious effects on one's self-esteem?

Confess.

"He who conceals his sins does not prosper, but whoever confesses and renounces them finds mercy" (Prov. 28:13).

But be careful how you do it.

Sometimes people wait until their guilt is so consuming that, in desperation for relief, they spill out their secret to the wrong ears and in wrong ways. They end up causing all kinds of hurt, sometimes more than the sin itself caused.

Confess your sins to God. If that is not sufficient, confess to a professional Christian counselor who can help you work through the questions of how and to whom further confession should be made.

HABITUAL SIN

Sin doesn't have to be a scandalous secret to devastate self-esteem. Paul is a good example. As mentioned in chapter five, Paul felt like his name was Powerless when he attempted to overcome his habitual sin. He wrote, "I have the desire to do what is good, but I cannot carry it out . . . the evil I do not want to do—this I keep doing. . . What a wretched man I am" (Rom. 7:18,19,24).

The habitual sin that troubled Paul was not some deep, dark thing. Many people would hardly have given this sin a second thought. God's law convicted Paul of the sin of covetousness, and that became a major problem for him (see Romans 7:7,8).

You may be caught in a similar dilemma. You are convicted of the sinfulness of some behavior. You ask God to forgive you, sincerely regret your transgression, and promise not to do it again. But you do.

As this pattern continues, you become more and more distressed and disgusted with yourself. You come to God with even more sorrow. You work up more determination that "this time" you will not fail. But again you do.

Eventually the wretched-man-that-I-am cry of Paul becomes yours as well. You are trapped with a terrible self-image.

Clearly, what's needed is to overcome the habitual sin. It is equally clear, though often missed, that you cannot do so by continuing your present pattern. It simply is not working. *Why would you continue an approach that does not work?*

What you need to know is that you are not condemned, however rotten you feel, and that God will give you strength to live differently (see Roman 8:1-4). This assurance eludes you so long as you have a fixation on your habitual sin. You have your mind, your attention, focused on the wrong thing.

"Those who live according to their sinful nature have their minds set on what that nature desires; but those who live in accordance with the Spirit have their minds set on what the Spirit desires" (Rom. 8:5).

You see, even repentance, sincere as it is, tends to set the defeated Christian's mind on the sinful nature and its desires. Unfortunately, some church fellowships are sin-oriented in much the same way. They place a tremendous emphasis on the world, the flesh, and the devil, and then wonder why they have trouble with all three constantly.

What is the solution? To stop repenting? No, but to repent after a godly fashion. The Bible talks about a repentance that doesn't need to be repented of, implying that there is both a wrong kind of repentance and a right kind (see 2 Corinthians 7:10).

Bruce Narramore and Bill Counts explain the contrast between good and bad repentance using the terms "psychological
guilt" and "constructive sorrow."

> Psychological guilt and constructive sorrow are very dif-
> ferent feelings. Psychological guilt . . . focuses largely on
> our past failures, our sense of wrongdoing, and our feel-
> ings of deserving punishment. . . . Constructive sorrow fo-
> cuses more on the persons we have injured. It is a very
> deep feeling but is not as concerned with our own failures
> as it is the damage done to others.
>
> *Psychological guilt produces self-inflicted misery. Con-*
> *structive sorrow produces a positive change of behavior.*
> Once the change in behavior comes, constructive sorrow
> vanishes. Its purpose is accomplished.[2]

This analysis reminds one of Alfred Adler's statement,
"Those who feel guilty have no intention of changing." Feeling
guilty can be a substitute for true repentance. It is a way of
punishing ourselves for wrongdoing instead of stopping the
behavior. On the other hand, those who have sincerely repented
have no need to feel guilty. They have been forgiven for past
sins and do not expect to continue them in the future.

When one repents, then, he must turn from the sin and from
the sorrow over it to the new way of living that God intends for
us. He must get his mind "set on what the Spirit desires."

As Paul put it after leaving his "wretched-man-that-I-am"
days behind, "Do not be overcome by evil, but overcome evil
with good" (Rom. 12:21).

That's it! Do you see?

Sin is to be crowded out, not by focusing on it but by replacing it with good. The same principle for living underlies the
familiar words, "Do not conform any longer to the pattern of
this world, but be transformed by the renewing of your mind"
(Rom. 12:2). In both passages, God's "do not" is followed by
"do," and it is the "do" that holds the secret of successfully

following through on the "do not."

Those who focus on nonconformity to the world fight a losing battle, often against shadows, because they have no adequate basis for being transformed. But those who are transformed by a renewed mind are also, by that very process, safeguarded against being conformed any longer to the world.

When we sin, we should see such behavior as uncharacteristic of us, not as proof that we are no good. Sin is a holdover from our old life which, Scripture teaches, is to be viewed as crucified, dead, and buried with Christ (see Romans 6:1-6). We are new people, called to a better and higher way, and it is this new way of the Spirit that must come to occupy our attention.[3]

WEAK-IN-THE-FLESH SIN

Not all sin is secret or habitual. Sometimes we are simply overtaken in a fault. We are tempted, perhaps in unusual circumstances, and we fall. This sin is not something we have nurtured in some dark, hidden place in our heart. It's not something we have done over and over. It might, in fact, be something we never imagined ourselves doing.

That's one reason weak-in-the-flesh sin is so damaging to our self-esteem. We believed that, hey, we're better people than to do something mean or hateful or perverted or whatever. Then we sin and prove we're not better people.

This is sometimes the experience of new or earnest Christians who love God and have no intention of dishonoring or displeasing him. When they realize they have sinned, they are acutely disappointed with themselves. They tried to fly but careened into the ground like a balloon crazily propelled by its own escaping air.

What went wrong?

They built their self-concept on an illusion. Scripture says, "Do not think of yourself more highly than you ought, but rather think of yourself with sober judgment" (Rom. 3:12).

This gets confusing because, as we have said, the mirror of

God's word encourages us to see ourselves as saints rather than sinners. We do so and then get unpleasantly reminded of the reality of our sinfulness.

That's what happened to Peter. We described in chapter five how Jesus gave him his name, which means Rock. This happened the first time they met. Three years later, the cross loomed before Jesus and we hear him saying that all the disciples will forsake him. Peter thinks, *Not me, I'm a Rock. Jesus said so, and I believe it, and that's what I'm determined to be*. So Peter says, "Though all men forsake you, yet will I not forsake you. I'll die first!"

Yet Peter did deny the Lord. The Rock was still capable of crumbling. Confronted with the reality of what happened, Peter went out and wept bitterly. His sin had devastated his self-esteem, and I imagine he contemplated suicide. However, Jesus had prayed for him that his faith would not fail, and he survived his dark hour of disillusionment.

Like us when we sin in the weakness of our flesh, Peter probably heard the sneering voice of Satan questioning whether there was anything at all to his profession of being a Christian. Jesus helped Peter work through that. Jesus asked Peter three times, "Do you love me?" (John 21:15). The question was increasingly a searching one, and Peter had to look deep within his heart in answering it. But the answer was yes. "Yes, Lord, you know that I love you" (John 21:16).

When that is our well-considered answer too, we have come a step closer to the sound judgment we are to have about ourselves. We are not yet all that Rock or Saint implies; we still have the weakness of our flesh to contend with; but we really do love the Lord.

GENERIC SIN

Secret sin, habitual sin, and weak-in-the-flesh sin can devastate self-esteem. So can sins that are an integral part of our nature as fallen human beings, our *generic sin*, to coin a phrase.

Generic sin refers to the pervasive deficit in our moral and spiritual condition that, quite apart from our yielding to any specific temptation, marks us as less than God's ideal. Paul wrote, "For all have sinned and fall short of the glory of God" (Rom. 3:23). It is this general "falling short" of God's glory to which we now look.

Generic sin is our failure to always love God with all our heart, soul, strength, and mind. It is our failure to always love our neighbors as ourselves. It is our failure to do all the good that we know we should do. It is our actions that are displeasing to God though we didn't intend them that way or even realize they were contrary to his will.

Question: *Are generic sins really sins?* If so, aren't we guilty all the time? If we are guilty all the time, can we ever have genuine self-esteem or true fellowship with a holy God?

The answers to these questions fall along two lines. We must either deny our real sinfulness at these points or deal with our sinfulness and find forgiveness.

Many deny it.

In the classic book, *Sin and Temptation*, first published in the mid-17th century, John Owen wrote, "The will is the cause of obedience or disobedience. Moral actions are willed. An ancient sage said, 'Every sin is so voluntary that if it is not voluntary it is not sin.'"

Dr. James Dobson says, "I personally believe no guilt should be considered to have come from God unless the behavior was an expression of willful disobedience." He cites an example of his son misunderstanding an order and doing the opposite of what was commanded. He excuses that and says, "You see, I judge my son more by his *intent* than by his actual behavior. . . . It is with great comfort that I rest in that same relationship with God."

Dr. Dobson gives the following example:

One mother whom I know walked toward a busy street with her three-year-old daughter. The little toddler ran ahead and stopped on the curb until her mother told her it was safe to cross. The woman was thinking about something else and nodded in approval when the little child asked, "Can I go now, Mommy?"

The youngster ran into the street and was struck full force by a semi-trailer truck. The mother gasped in terror as she watched the front and back wheels of the truck crush the life from her precious little girl. The hysterical woman, screaming in anguish and grief, ran to the road and gathered the broken remains of the child in her arms. She had killed her own daughter who depended on her for safety. This mother will *never* escape the guilt of that moment.

The "video tape recording" has been rerun a million times in her tormented mind—picturing a trusting baby asking her mother if it was safe to cross the street. Clearly, God has not placed that guilt on the heartbroken woman, but her suffering is no less real.[4]

Dobson says this woman's guilt is not "from God," but he also says she will never escape it and the real suffering it entails. That's the trouble with the "not guilty" approach; it often does not solve the problem.

It also does not square with Scripture, as I have written elsewhere:

Scripture teaches that wrongdoing is sin whether we choose, will, or intend wrong or not. In fact, our wrongdoing is still sin when, far from willing it, we don't even know we did wrong. Leviticus 4 and 5 deals with many such situations. One verse sums up much of the teaching: "If a person sins and does what is forbidden in any of the Lord's commands, even though he does not know it, he is guilty and will be held responsible" (5:17). The sixteenth verse speaks of making restitution "for what he has failed to do," suggesting that sins of omission are also sins whether intended or not.[5]

Generic sins are sins, but Jesus died for our sins, and his perfect righteousness has been put to our account if we trust in him. Our guilt is removed not by denying we have done wrong but by appropriating the grace of God that is ours through our Lord Jesus Christ.

A strange phenomenon exists among Christians whereby we are much more willing to admit that we are sinners than that we have sinned. We come to the Lord initially like the publican who beat upon his breast and said, "God, be merciful to me a sinner." Then we spend the rest of our lives trying to deny what we have already confessed. When the Spirit nudges us about some wrong action or attitude, we defend ourselves, rationalize, and do everything but admit we sinned.

You cannot get anywhere in an area of your life in which you are bogged down arguing about whether or not you have sinned. My own counsel to the woman whose child was killed in traffic would be not to argue when her heart accuses her. Instead, she should thank the Lord Jesus that he died to take away all her guilt and that nothing remains in any account against her. She is blameless, not in her own good intentions, but in Christ.

Battered women and sexually abused women and children often get into trouble at this point, too. Battered women often feel they have frustrated and aggravated their partners or somehow failed to meet their needs. Sexually abused children may feel they have seduced or at least cooperated with the adult who had sex with them. This is generic sin condemning them.

We rush to assure such people that they are not at fault; they are victims, not wrongdoers. It is true that they are victims. It is true that there is no excuse or justifications whatever for their abuse.

However, there is good reason for them to feel guilty. Truly innocent people are hard to find. We've only had one on earth, and he left for heaven almost two thousand years ago.

If you have been abused and are totally innocent in the relationship, fine. Assert your innocence. But if you can't seem to get free of guilt, rather than trying by sheer will power to exonerate yourself, go ahead and confess that you are not all you ought to be, and you have not always done right, even in the relationship in question. Also, recognize clearly that your wrongdoing, whatever it was, in no way justified your being abused, and in Christ you are fully forgiven.

THE SIN THAT NEVER WAS

In talking about generic sin, I have urged that a willingness to confess sin rather than argue about it is a step toward putting the whole thing behind us. However, there is also such a thing as false guilt. False guilt does not occur when we have done wrong unintentionally. It occurs when we have not done wrong, but our heart accuses us anyhow.

This is likely to happen anytime we behave contrary to the way we have been taught, regardless of whether our action are right or wrong. Many people also feel guilty whenever they are accused of anything, even if they haven't done it.

Bruce Narramore and Bill Counts write:

Most of us feel guilty over a number of things God doesn't consider sin.

I often encounter college students whose parents are absolutely determined their children get college degrees. Sometime during their college years the students wake up to the fact they don't want to be in college. They would prefer to marry or enter a vocation that doesn't require college education. Yet as soon as they consider "dropping out" they start feeling guilty. They're afraid they're letting their parents down. Later if they do drop out, they may repeatedly be haunted by the thought that they made the wrong decision. When a girl in this situation marries, she often starts resenting her husband for "depriving her of an education or profession."

In similar ways, we all feel guilty over some less-than-perfect ideals. Some women feel guilty if their homes aren't spotless. Some of us feel guilty if we have nice things, and others feel guilty if we don't. Still others feel guilty if they don't say yes to every request to serve in their church or social organization.

But the Bible doesn't say every American should get a college degree, have a spotless home, teach a Sunday school class or work sixteen hours a day. Many people who battle guilt are not doing wrong; they are condemning themselves for failing to live up to their ideal self—the borrowed standards of their parents or society.[6]

How do you deal with false guilt?

Basically, you do it by believing God instead of your condemning conscience. If you have resolved some question of right or wrong by consulting God, if he has given approval to your course of action, you say to your conscience, "You are wrong. I am not going to listen to your accusations."

As the Scripture says, "Whenever our conscience condemns us, God is greater than our conscience and knows everything" (1 John 3:20, Beck).

GO AND SIN NO MORE

It's too bad so many Christians allow sin to beat them into the dust of self-reproach and shame. It is so unnecessary. In Christ, we are in a truly enviable position as regards guilt. As the apostle Paul puts it, "Therefore, there is now no condemnation for those who are in Christ Jesus" (Rom. 8:1).

No condemnation! If you are a Christian and feel condemned, you know that feeling is not from God.

Because of Christ, you can stand free and unashamed in the presence of both man and God. Nowhere is this pictured more clearly than in the account in John 8 of the woman taken in adultery. There was no question of her guilt for she was caught in the very act. What did Jesus say when confronted with this sinful woman by her accusers? He told them, "If any one of you is without sin, let him be the first to throw a stone at her" (v. 7).

We read, "At this, those who heard began to go away one at a time, the older ones first" (v. 9). I've always wondered about that. Why the older ones? I don't know whether they were "dirty old men" and more guilty than the younger ones or whether they were just quicker to acknowledge their own guilt. Maybe it was both.

In any case, when they had all gone, Jesus said, "Woman, where are they? Has no one condemned you?"

"No one, sir," she said.

"Then neither do I condemn you," Jesus declared. "Go now and leave your life of sin" (vv. 10-12).

We, like this woman, are guilty without a doubt when our lives are stacked against the perfect demands of God's law. Yet no man is qualified to condemn us, for they all are as surely guilty as we. That leaves us standing before Jesus alone. What does he say? "Neither do I condemn you."

Praise God! Man *cannot* condemn us, and the Lord *will not.* We are free.

Someone may object that this gives a license to sin. No, Jesus says to us as he said to the woman, "Go now and leave your life of sin" (v. 11).

Did she?

Will we?

Yes.

We still won't be perfect, of course, but we will be free. Free from the driven, confused, sin-centered existence that has been our downfall all along until now. Free to begin living out the new life in the Spirit that we wanted when we sincerely repented and promised God we would do his will. Free to know we aren't wretches.

We are beloved children who have come home.

TIME TO CONSIDER

1. How do people act when their self-esteem is damaged by sin? What did Adam and Eve do? How do guilty children behave?

2. Do you think most Christians tend to:
   a. feel too guilty?
   b. not feel guilty enough?
   c. other (explain)
Are you similar or different from most Christians in this regard?

3. If anyone has "skeletons in the closet," secret sins known only to God, should that person confess to someone else even if it's past history? Should confession always be made to the person sinned against—a husband, for instance? Why or why not?

4. How do Christians often try "more of the same" when their struggle with habitual sin is a losing one? What principles can help one overcome habitual sin? Is it necessary to go through a process that leaves you desperate before you can find help? Why or why not?

5. How can we view ourselves both as Saints (who aren't expected to sin) and as weak-in-the-flesh people (who are expected to sin)? How does Romans 12:3 relate to this issue?

6. How would you explain what I call a phenomenon "whereby we are much more willing to admit that we are sinners than that we have sinned." Would healthy self-esteem make people more likely or less likely to admit sin? Why?

7. How does Jesus' acceptance of us set us free from shame? How would you relate Romans 8:33,34 to this question and to the story of the adulterous woman (John 8:1-11)?

9
...

Frustration: Failing in Our Endeavors

Sin is one form of failure that can seriously damage our self-esteem, but it is not the only one. We may fail in an endeavor and be totally innocent of any wrongdoing. We *know* we haven't sinned. Yet we feel disgusted with ourselves because we attempted something, and it didn't turn out as we hoped. We failed.

Such experiences are not exclusive to incompetent people. They are common to all who aspire to achievement of any kind. Failing is part of the price of *doing* and can be avoided only by a profound withdrawal that is tantamount to resigning from life. And that, of course, is the biggest failure of all.

Some failures are more crucial than others and have more far-reaching effects, but all failure hurts. In this chapter, we'll consider the damage to self-esteem that results from "little failures" and "big failures" and try to suggest some help for both.

LITTLE FAILURES—BIG WOUNDS

Craig Selness tells the following story of a failure he experienced as a boy:

Our class was having a spelling bee against another class down the hall. My teacher and my classmates were all counting on me, their champion speller, to lead them to glorious victory.

But early in the game, I choked. The teacher asked me to spell *prophet*, like the ones in the Bible. But the only word I could picture in my mind was spelled p-r-o-f-i-t. To the groans of my classmates, the loud cheers of the other team, and the obvious disappointment of my teacher who had such high expectations of me, I had failed. I had let them down.

I ran to my desk and buried my head in my arms, tears streaking my face. It was a wound that hurt deeply and which took a long time to heal.[1]

The story illustrates how even a good student can fail and feel worthless as a result. The poor student, who has to contend with failure regularly, has just that much more to overcome.

A child may get poor grades because of a learning disability, a hearing or vision problem, or for some other reason that's not his fault. Still, because he hasn't performed well, he is likely to feel unworthy and unacceptable.

Some children are mislabeled "poor student" simply because they have gotten crossways of the system at some point, like Levauna, whose experience was described in chapter seven. Having failed conspicuously somewhere along the line, they are now identified as failures both by others and by themselves.

SOMEBODY TO BELIEVE IN US

We are often caught in a vicious circle. We fail. As a result, people downgrade us, our confidence is destroyed, and our self-esteem is damaged. This, in turn, keeps us from attempting other things or causes us to try halfheartedly or predisposes us to fail again.

But if someone believes in us, we are encouraged to believe in ourselves as well. Unfortunately, finding people who will believe in you when you are a "failure" is not easy. Often mothers believe in us, but we tend to discount their belief as unjustified.

I have good news.

Somebody does believe in you.

It is the very one who has asked you to believe in him.

God believes in you and because he does, you can believe in yourself. God made you and endowed you with capabilities and potential. How you compare with other people he made and endowed doesn't matter, for he only expects performance from you commensurate with your endowments.

Would a just God create you incapable of flying and then reproach you because you can't fly? No. But he would be displeased with you if you could walk but won't. I say he'd be displeased, but his displeasure would largely be over *what you are missing in life* when you won't walk. He wants us to live abundantly.

God did not make you to be beaten down by failure. If the limits on your ability are from him, accept them, and accept yourself as he does. If they are not from him but are imposed on you because of past failure, remember that he believes in you because he knows what is possible for you. He's just waiting for you to shake off your self-pity and unbelief and start moving.

It has been well said that failure is a word describing an event, not a person. You may have failed, but that doesn't mean you are a failure. Though a particular course or undertaking of yours failed, *you* are still a beautiful creation of God.

GOD IS BIGGER THAN YOU THINK

No matter how many times you have failed, or how desperately, there is hope with God. Not just a glimmer of hope, but a bright and shining hope that you are becoming God's person. Christians have been known to wail and cry about having "missed the will of God," as if some fateful failure of the past now dooms them to failure forever. That's mostly nonsense. We've all missed the will of God because we have all sinned. God is neither unforgiving nor unresourceful, and he can overrule our failures.

Nobody ever failed more as an individual than Israel did as a nation. Because of Israel's sin and failure, ancient prophets not only pronounced judgment of God on the nation, but also sometimes despaired of any hope for her future. About the judgment for sin, they were right. About no hope for the future, they were wrong, and God told them so.

God sent one of his prophets, Jeremiah, down to the house of the potter to learn this lesson. There Jeremiah saw a significant thing. "The pot he was shaping from the clay was marred in his hands; so the potter formed it into another pot, shaping it as seemed best to him" (Jer. 18:4).

God is not so lacking in creativity that he cannot think of anything worthwhile to do with a lump of human clay that has shown some defects as he has worked with it. He is quite able to fashion another vessel that seems good to him. *Good* to him. Not just passable, but good in the eyes of God.

God says he can make you a good, new vessel.

So then, failure isn't fatal—necessarily. Not if you look beyond the failure and believe in yourself anyhow, as God does.

FALSE FAILURE

One fault I have largely overcome is berating myself for failing to accomplish things as easily and quickly as I would like. Typically, such self-talk went like this: "I don't believe it! This is a simple task any two-year-old ought to be able to do in five minutes, and I suppose I'm going to spend half the day on it."

Of course, I didn't believe what I was saying. Mostly, I was letting off steam. Sometimes, if the product was poorly designed, I would rail against the manufacturer instead of myself.

"There's absolutely no excuse for this. Anybody who would design such a monstrosity ought to be shot." Usually, though, I have had to battle the feeling that I, in some measure, am at fault.

Any failure is likely to bring with it a sense of self-reproach, regardless of the cause. To prove this to yourself, conduct a simple experiment. Break the handle off a cup. Then carefully glue it back on with weak glue that will not hold much weight. Now serve a cup of coffee to some unsuspecting guest. Be sure it's not too hot, though, and that your guest is not wearing fine clothes because you know what's going to happen. When she picks it up and the handle breaks and coffee spills everywhere, watch her reactions.

If the person knows of your trickery, she will either be angry at you or amused at the incident. Since she does not know, however, she will likely be full of apologies and act as if she is at fault even though all she did was pick up her cup of coffee.

In other words, just as there is false guilt (see chapter eight), there is also *false failure*. Don't be too quick to assume you failed somehow. You may have been working with a broken cup.

FAILURE AS A LEARNING DEVICE

If you have ever searched the help wanted columns of the newspaper, you have seen the frequent stipulation that applicants have experience. Employers know that proficiency in almost any job requires certain skills gained only by experience and practice.

Experience involves failure. That's why the employer demands an experienced worker. He wants one who has already made his mistakes somewhere else and has learned to do the work correctly.

Failure, then, is a learning device. If we learn from our failures, they are not a total loss.

SET MULTIPLE REALISTIC GOALS

Failure or success is a somewhat subjective thing. No one can appropriately attach either label to your endeavors unless they know what your goals are. Ordinarily, you are the one who should decide that.

Suppose I were to enter the twenty-six-mile Boston Marathon. You are an acquaintance of mine and you are waiting at the finish line to see how I do. At last the front runners come into view and I am not among them. *Too bad,* you think, *the poor guy not only won't win but he isn't even among the top ten contenders. What a failure!*

About an hour later, I come staggering across the finish line. You are groping for something to say to console me, but then you notice I don't need consoling. I am extremely pleased with my performance. It turns out that I didn't enter to win. My goal was to finish, and I have succeeded.

I might have set a number of other "lesser" goals as well. Simply to make the trip to Boston and enter the marathon could have been my goal. But my example to encourage a hesitant friend of mine with far more potential than me to take up long-distance running could have been my goal.

Now, if I accomplish what I set out to do, can that be considered a failure? That's what I'd call a success.

Thomas Edison is said to have conducted some 18,000 experiments in developing the electric light bulb. Does that mean he failed 17,999 times? Not at all. When he tried a platinum filament and it quickly burned out, he had succeeded in eliminating that design. His other experiments similarly succeeded in eliminating other possibilities. His ultimate goal was an electric light bulb, but his intermediate goals were many.

The time to think about your goals is before you begin. There may be occasions when you will decide that you should undertake some endeavor the "success" of which is unlikely. You may want to enter some race you have little realistic hope of winning. OK, be clear about that at the beginning. Identify the things you do hope to accomplish. Then your heart will not call failure what was really a noble success.

DON'T LET FAILURE HAVE THE LAST WORD

Failure is temporary. One may fail at something many times but wipe out the negative effect by later succeeding.

Last year we sold a house. We did it ourselves without the aid of a realtor. The first people who phoned in response to our "For Sale" sign did not buy the place. In fact, they didn't even show up at the appointed time to inspect it. The first time we advertised it in the newspaper, it didn't sell either. Nor the second time. Nor the third.

We might have given up. We might have accepted failure and turned the house over to professionals, but we'd been this route before. We knew they had no magic and that in the seller's market existing at the time, we could sell the place if the price was right.

We did. We turned down a number of unsatisfactory offers. Several prospective buyers disappointed us by deciding against the purchase. But after two months, the right people came along with the right offer, and we had a sale. All the failures meant nothing.

We need to take a positive but realistic view of failure. I have suggested some reasons to take courage and be hopeful, no matter what our failures have been.

Nothing I have said, however, implies that it is wrong to feel bad about failing.

Unwavering faith in God rules our despair, but it does not exempt us from sorrow. It's all right to cry over spilt milk. It's OK to hate it when you fail. What is not OK is to hate yourself, to keep feeling guilty when you've been forgiven, to cry so long and hard over spilt milk that you're unable to clean up the mess and go on.

You see, it's the finish that counts, and you are not finished yet. Not unless you are dead.

It was the night before the intercollegiate games. I was a freshman at Yale. The Captain stood under my room on the

111

fifth floor of old North and called up to me that I was to run the mile the next day at Berkeley Oval in New York. That shout in the dark gave me one of the greatest thrills of my life.

Two o'clock the following afternoon found me in the Yale training quarters. The Captain, ostentatiously cool and collected, told me that Yale, the Freshman Class, and nearly all right-minded civilized people were anxious to have me win the Mile that day. I was entirely willing to oblige them.

Then old Mike Murphy, the best trainer the world has ever known, muttered some advice in my ear about not getting pocketed and laying back until the last quarter.

"Get set," the starter shouted. Then came the bang of a pistol—and we were off.

One of the boys who ran that day was an almost unknown runner, representing a small school. At the first corner, while fighting for the lead, he was accidentally spiked and thrown headlong. One of his legs was gashed by the long spikes on the shoes of another competitor, and his hands and face were cut by the cinders. By the time he had struggled to his feet, the whole field was thirty yards ahead. . . .

It seemed hopeless for him to go on; nevertheless he started after the crowd of runners as bravely as if nothing had happened.

All around the first lap he remained behind them all. Little by little, however, he began to cut down the lead of runners nearest him, and by the end of the first half he was up among the laggards of the race, twenty yards back of the leaders.

Then came that bitter third quarter. Nothing is harder in athletics than the third quarter of a fast mile. One has already run a half at full speed, and there is still another quarter to come. An iron band seems to tighten around one's chest. There is the salt taste of blood in the mouth, and one longs to give up, and fall down and rest.

The pacemakers had reached the fourth quarter, and a deep-toned bell signalled the beginning of the last lap, while the cheers of the crowd swept across the track like a storm.

The sound was like a spur to the speed of that boy who had been last. He shot by a little group of runners, and in the backstretch was hard upon the heels of the four leaders. As they swung around the last corner into the homestretch, those four who were in front heard the sound of flying feet approaching them from behind, and knew that the race that day was to be fought out by five instead of four.

As all five of them swung into the homestretch, the spectators leaned forward from the stands and called upon the runners by name for one last desperate effort. No one called on the boy who ran last of that quintette, nor even knew his name.

Suddenly, level with the fourth man, came the blackened, gashed face of the last runner, and slowly drew away from him.

Now the finish was only thirty yards away, and suddenly beside the third man showed that same disfigured face, whose staring eyes saw nothing but the goal. That third man did his best and gave all he had to hold his place—I ought to know, I was that third man—but slowly and surely the boy who had fallen at the start drew away from him.

Then he challenged the other two, who were running neck and neck, and five yards from the finish drew even with them. For an instant that seemed a year the three struggled for the lead, and then, at the very finish, the runner who had been left lying prostrate in the dirt when the race began, threw himself forward, broke the tape a scant inch ahead of the other two, won the race, and broke the Intercollegiate Record for the Mile.

In forty years of athletics I have never seen again so

113

gallant a finish, and to the day of my death will never forget that race nor that runner.

In the lives of all of us there are times when we stumble and fall and are defiled by the dirt, and cut and gashed and hurt. Yet we are beaten only if we give up and lie down hopeless and helpless. No matter how far the fall or how dreadful the failure, there is only one thing to do—get up and go on and on and never, never quit! The start is important, but—it's the finish that wins![2]

TIME TO CONSIDER

1. Have you ever had anyone in your life who greatly believed in you despite your failings? How much did that mean to you? Who might you encourage in the same way?

2. How can a person who has missed God's will—maybe married unwisely, chosen the wrong vocation, acquired an addiction—ever escape failure?

3. How common is false failure? Can you think of a situation in which you blamed yourself when you were not at fault?

4. What is an example of a failure that became a learning device for you? How else could you have learned the same thing? What are some positive character traits people can acquire from failure? What will determine whether your failures make you bitter or better?

5. What are some ways to program successes into your life, thereby taking the edge off of your failures?

6. Think of the projects you are now engaged in or anticipating. How can you set multiple goals so that, even if a project is not a total success, it will not be a total failure?

10

...

Alienation: Failing in Our Relationships

Can anything tear us up more than being trapped in a hurting or broken relationship? For most people, the answer is all too painfully clear. Nothing is harder, nothing is worse.

John Powell writes:

Only recently have the behavioral sciences reached the point of enlightenment to show us that unconditional love is the only soil in which the seed of a human person can grow.[1]

Unconditional love is *the only soil* in which human personality can grow? If that's true, it's no wonder we feel like uprooted plants, dying on the vine, when our relationships are wrong.

Powell also writes, in the same book:

The most perceptive insight of contemporary personalism

is that I become a person only if I receive my personhood from someone else through the gift of affirmation. If I never see myself valued by others, I will never value myself. To this the psychiatrist Victor Frankl enjoins the absolutely necessary advice: True self-esteem and a true sense of identity can be found only in the reflected appraisal of those whom we have loved.[2]

In what could seem to be a conflicting vein, we have said that a self-image based on feedback from other people, while very common, is faulty. Our theme has been that a correct self-concept must come from God instead of from "the world."

It may be true that "I become a person only if I receive my personhood from someone else through the gift of affirmation." However, that "someone else" may be, should be, and for some deprived people *must* be God. Otherwise, if the important people in our lives disavow our worth, we are hopeless, doomed to a life of self-reproach and non-personhood.

Affirmation from those closest to us helps. But if we say it's essential, we offer no hope to those who simply don't get such affirmation but, to the contrary, are continually degraded.

I believe there is hope. The experience of Robby and his sister, told in chapter six, constitutes evidence that God can get through to people personally and directly with the assurance that he loves them. It may take a crisis, and the message from God may want reinforcement from loving people later. Still, God does touch people who feel worthless. He does let downcast people know that, to him, they are of great value.

Sharon Johnson had such an experience. Because God himself got through to her when she had no one else, she was rescued from self-reproachful suicide. She writes:

My head throbbed and nausea swept over me. I was nearly unconscious at last, my knees weak and trembling as I stood near the exhaust of my car in our closed garage.

Why is it taking so long? I wondered. The stench of

exhaust fumes filled my head and I detested the sick feeling in my stomach. I hadn't read about that, and for a moment I felt angry that this information had been denied me.

The traumas of the past few months flashed before me. My husband's affair with another woman, the sordid details haunting me constantly; his rejection of me in favor of her; my children's accusations against me in their painful separation from their dad, who had misled them about the reasons for his departure.

In the end, I'd simply had no strength left. My husband was right, I told myself. I had failed to make him happy. I had failed my children. They would be much better off in the care of someone else. The physical beatings my husband had given me—I supposed I'd deserved those too.

My mind had been foggy for days now. Half-empty cups, poured and forgotten, sat in various places throughout the house. Dirty dishes filled the sink at the end of the day. *Had I fed the children or were they yesterday's dishes?* I couldn't remember.

Why had God given my children to me, a failure? I would remember to ask Him that. All I wanted at this moment was to be with Jesus, to feel His arms around me.

Suddenly a movement jarred my thoughts back to the present. I realized my knees had buckled and I reached out to the car for support. Knowing time was short, I attempted to form a mental picture of God welcoming me into heaven. Something wasn't right. I felt like a child being scolded.

"Do you really want to face Me this way?" a voice spoke softly into my mind. *Reality hit me like a bullet. God loves me! He wants me alive. Obedience will bring me into eternity in His timing, not mine.*

I reached for the garage door. My body responded slowly. My hand felt like jelly as it hit the door and moved downward to the handle. I gripped it and pulled, but it wouldn't move. *Locked!*

117

The smoke-filled air burned my eyes and I couldn't see. Was I to die here, my choice to take my life being confirmed even though I had changed my mind? In panic I prayed, "Lord, forgive me!"

The latch snapped open in my hand, and when I yanked, the door went up quickly. Bright sunlight mixed with the polluted air as I tried to adjust my vision to the surroundings. There was my neighbor's house across the street. The sky was blue and clear and the yard fresh and green. The rhododendron bush was in bloom, its pink and purple blossoms gently nodding in the breeze.

The faces of my three beautiful daughters flashed to mind. *God had trusted me as their mother, husband or not.* I could raise them with His help.

That simple affirmation was the beginning of a new self-image and a new life for me. My progress has been slow at times and the lessons many since that day nine years ago. Sometimes I take one step forward and two back, but less and less frequently. Verses such as 1 John 4:4 help: "Greater is He that is in you than he that is in the world." God is in me, and that, not some other person's approval, makes me worthwhile. Never again will I allow another human being to control my sense of self-worth.

Looking back I ask why I ever allowed myself to dwell on my failures. Then I realize that my mistake was in making my husband lord of my life. My self-esteem for eleven years was dependent on him. His acceptance and approval governed my opinion of myself completely, until my eyes were opened to this error.

Today my heart aches for those in bondage in situations similar to mine. Wives cringe as I did when orders are yelled at them by unloving husbands. With their confidence crushed by harsh words and name-calling, they feel worthless, condemned both by others and by themselves. How I pray that God's love and acceptance will get through to them!

To the rejected, I would say: remember, the perfect Jesus was condemned and rejected too. Yet God said, "This is My beloved Son, in whom I am well pleased." If we have trusted in Jesus Christ, we are a 10 in God's eyes though we fail daily, for He sees the final product—His image perfectly reflected in us.[3]

These days more and more marriages fail. We're often told there is really no "innocent party" in such cases. Both partners have contributed to the breakdown of marriage. Perhaps so, but that very attitude is a put down and can complicate the self-esteem problem for the divorced person. He or she gets the message: *you have failed, permanently.* Never mind if your mate was hooked on drugs or alcohol, abused you physically and verbally, or turned out to be a homosexual both in tendency and practice.

The teaching of some Christians aggravates the problem by stating or implying that it takes only one partner to make a marriage work. Women especially are led to believe that if they are submissive enough and spiritual enough their husbands will be transformed. This claim is usually supported with glowing success stories of women who did it. The teaching serves only to beat down those who find it doesn't work that way for them—even though they try it, perhaps for years.

Put downs and failure get all mixed together in situations like this. We don't know how much of our bad feeling about ourselves comes from others' attitudes and how much from our own sense of failure. Either way, our self-esteem is devastated.

OTHER TYPES OF REJECTION

A troubled relationship can damage us even if it is not such an important and intimate one as marriage. Any time we sense rejection from another person, we tend to feel failure because we want people to like us. We want them to think well of us. More important, we want to think well of ourselves, and when someone else shows he does not think well of us, we are afraid he might be right.

This is what wipes out many sales people. They can't take the rejection. They tell themselves that the prospect's refusal to purchase is no reflection on them, but they have a hard time believing it.

I asked my friend Tom Mullins, a trainer of sales people, how much rejection a person can take. "The average person can't take any," he said, to my surprise. "Reject him once and it's all over. He crashes in flames."

We all know people whose lives seem to contradict that evaluation—children who keep bidding for affirmation and attention from unresponsive parents, wives who keep talking at husbands who aren't listening, and husbands who keep trying to buy their wives' affections. But in these cases, the rejected person is also a trapped and desperate person with little choice but to keep trying.

When a close relationship already exists, people swallow rejection and perservere in the relationship partly because, as we've said, failing in relationships is so painful and threatening. But by the same token, people ordinarily steer clear of new relationships that seem headed for difficulty. At the first hint of rejection from someone we're not already tied to, we turn away.

Many times, if a neighbor snubs us once, that's it. He won't get a second chance. We don't need any more rejection that will only make us feel bad about ourselves. As a result of initial failure in reaching out to people, we often withdraw. To the degree such withdrawl becomes typical of us, it isolates us from other people. This is detrimental to our self-esteem almost as much as rejection. We come to see ourselves as not adept at making friends and therefore not likable.

Withdrawing is detrimental to our personal growth because it is often in relating to others that we grow the most. Each of us needs one close friend with whom we can relate freely, openly, and honestly. But what if you are caught in your isolation? What if you are a loner? What can you do about it?

One possibility is to join a warm, accepting, and supportive group. Too often, other dynamics prevent the development of this kind of relationship. Just getting two or more people together won't do it. As Paul wrote to the Corinthians, their get-togethers, even at their love feasts, were more damaging than helpful (see 1 Corinthians 11:17).

What keeps our relationships from becoming the mutual benefit and blessing that we all need them to be?

PLAYING TOP DOG

Roberta has an intimidating style of relating to others that has developed over long years. Actually, it is a neurotic device to bolster her self-esteem, though Roberta doesn't have the remotest clue to that fact.

Her behavior consists of immediately seeking to establish herself in a superior position each time you meet her. She has numerous techniques for doing this—all refined to an art.

Her favorite tactic is to make a comment or ask a question that puts you on the defensive. She does this good-naturedly, but that's just to mask the purpose of it.

Roberta says things like, "Hey, I didn't see you in church last Sunday." If someone else said that to you, it might be a wholesome expression of interest, a way of letting you know you were missed. Roberta's purpose is something else altogether. You are now supposed to explain to her why you were not in church. The reasons you offer don't matter. The point is that you are in a position of answering to her for your actions, as if you were some sort of underling. Or Roberta may greet you with, "Where's your wife? Left her home again, huh?" Once more, what you explain doesn't matter. Now you're accounting to her for your personal home life.

Looking at her watch as you arrive, Roberta may say, "I expected you a little earlier." She will follow that up with some specious reason the exact time of your arrival matters. If you are even one minute late, you are supposed to be apologetic. If you are actually on time, you are supposed to feel like you should have been early. Either way, you are to defer to the top dog.

Had you come earlier, however, you may be sure Roberta would have said something intimidating about that. It's not what *you* do that is the problem; it's Roberta's need to play top dog.

If you know someone who constantly makes you feel inferior or on trial, try to detach yourself enough to observe the interaction between the two of you. You may well find someone is playing top dog with you.

What can you do about it? Several things.

First, recognizing what's happening—and why and how—can help you put things in perspective. Realizing that the other person has an emotional malfunction and that it's more his problem than yours takes a lot of the pain out of the situation.

Second, if you can't handle the continual intimidation, you may want to limit the relationship.

Third, you can challenge the behavior. To come right out and accuse a person of playing top dog may alienate him, but the relationship is already dismal so you don't have a lot to lose. However, a better way might be simply to stop playing his game. When he comes at you with top-dog tactics, don't lie down and roll over.

You might say, "Let's not begin our visit with me explaining or defending myself. It makes me feel as if you are finding fault with me. That's not your intention, is it?"

One or two encounters like that and top dog will probably change his treatment of you—let up a little. He might even pause to reflect on what his habitual behavior says about him.

BEING A VICTIM

Another negative way of relating is as a victim. Dr. Wayne Dyer has written of this at length:

Think back to the very first time your spouse abused you, by raising his voice, getting angry, hitting you, or whatever. . . .

Suppose that instead of being shocked, stunned, afraid or tearful, you had showed your partner your hand, told him that it was a registered weapon, and given him a solid karate chop to the stomach, followed up with, "I don't intend to take that kind of abuse from you. I think of myself as a person with dignity, and I'm not ever going to be shoved around by you or anyone else. Please give yourself a heavy dose of second thoughts before you try something like that again. That's all I have to say about it." And then you proceeded to carry on an intelligent conversation.

While this may seem an absurd thing to imagine, it illustrates the point: Had you reacted from strength and firm intolerance for abusive behavior right from the beginning, you would once and for all have taught your partner something very important—that you will not indulge such nasty behavior for one second.

But your reaction was probably disastrously different. Whether you cried, acted hurt or insulted, or showed fear, you sent out a fatal signal that you would not necessarily like the way he was treating you, but that you would take it, and even more significantly, that you would let yourself be manipulated emotionally by it.

When I told Gayle this theory she said, "I could never have reacted anything like the way you say I might have!" At first she wanted to defend her entrenched position that her husband and her children were totally at fault for her victim status, and she wanted me to feel sorry for her and become an ally in her misery. When I persisted in stating that the "karate chop" doesn't need violence, physical or any other kind, to have its psychological impact, and that she might have left the room, refused to talk with him, or even called the police, to illustrate her intolerance, she began to get the message. She soon accepted the fact that she had indeed taught almost everyone that she was willing to be a "dumpee," and she resolved to work at changing from then on.[4]

Some may feel it's "not Christian" to stand up for one's dignity as Dyer suggests. To the contrary, failing to do so is what's not Christian because it is inconsistent with love. No one should be either a victim or a victimizer. If you are a victim, and you allow such a sinful relationship to continue, you are doing a decided disservice to everyone involved.

AS A CARDBOARD CHARACTER

A third counter-productive way of relating is to do so superficially. This means refusing to be open and real with others in our lives. When this happens, people deal with one another as cardboard characters instead of flesh and blood human beings.

John Powell gives an example of the dramatic improvement that can come when superficiality yields to openness.

Tommy, one of his former university students, came down with terminal cancer. Tommy said:

"I decided to spend what time I had left doing something more profitable. I thought about you and your class and I remembered something else you had said: 'The essential sadness is to go through life without loving. But it would be equally sad to go through life and leave this world without ever telling those you loved that you had loved them.'

"So I began with the hardest one: my dad. He was reading the newspaper when I approached him."

"Dad. . . ."

"Yes, what?" he asked without lowering the newspaper.

"Dad, I would like to talk with you."

"Well, talk."

"I mean. . . . It's really important."

The newspaper came down three slow inches. "What is it?"

"Dad, I love you. I just wanted you to know that."

Tom smiled at me and said with obvious satisfaction, as though he felt a warm and secret joy flowing inside of him: "The newspaper fluttered to the floor. Then my father did two things I could never remember him ever doing before. He cried and he hugged me. And we talked all night, even though he had to go to work the next morning. It felt so good to be close to my father, to see his tears, to feel his hug, to hear him say that he loved me.

"It was easier with my mother and little brother. They cried with me, too, and we hugged each other, and started saying real nice things to each other. We shared the things we had been keeping secret for so many years. I was only sorry about one thing: that I had waited too long. Here I was, in the shadow of death, and I was just beginning to open up to all the people I had actually been close to."[5]

In your relationships, commit yourself to overcoming and eliminating those styles that are harmful: playing top dog/bottom dog, being a victim or a victimizer, being a closed person so that you are like a cardboard character whom no one can get close to.

Embrace a new vision of the person you can be, one who in your relationships to others:

- *is easy and comfortable to be around* because you are comfortable with yourself.
- *inspires the trust of others* because you need no hidden self-boosting agenda and have none.
- *commands respect* because you respect both yourself and others out of reverence for Christ.
- *honestly loves and cares for others* because in Christ you are no longer an empty vessel with no love to give.

Let this vision live in your heart and mind. Reach for it. Believe it can be. When you see it embodied in another, thank God, and renew your fervent prayer for the same grace. When you see something in yourself alien to the vision, renounce it, and thank God for showing you the things you need to put away. Do these things, and you will surely look back one day and see that God has done something wonderful; he has made you like unto the vision.

TIME TO CONSIDER

1. Privately make a list of six to ten people who touch your life in meaningful ways: family members, friends, coworkers, Christian leaders. On a separate sheet of paper, place a star in the center representing yourself. Then work down your list and for each person from whom you feel lack of acceptance, place an X on the paper, for those with whom you feel acceptance, place an O. Locate the Xs and Os close to or further from the star according to how close these people are to you.

2. Analyze your chart. Share it with others, and discuss its meaning as you feel it's appropriate. (Do not share the list of names, only the chart of symbols.) If you added a symbol representing the Lord (a cross), where would you locate it on your chart? Would you enclose it in an O, symbolizing that you feel accepted by the Lord? Or put an X through it, symbolizing non-acceptance?

3. Why would anyone let a friend or relative be top dog? Why do women sometimes allow their husbands or children to victimize them? Why is it never right to permit victimization to continue? How can women deal with the problem?

4. How easy or difficult is it for you to verbalize your love and other emotions to family members and friends? How can one express love other than verbally, and are such non-verbal expressions enough? When does saying "I love you" become manipulative? Are men who batter their wives sometimes sweet, romantic, and verbal about their love?

5. What vision do you have for yourself as a lover of people? What changes do you need to make to fulfill your vision?

Part IV

Performance Counts

11
...

Achievement
Is for Everyone,
Isn't It?

Do you agree or disagree with the following statement? "Self-esteem should be based entirely on *being* or identity and not at all on behavior or performance."

Perhaps you aren't sure you understand the statement clearly enough to agree or disagree. The following passage spells out much the same proposition. See whether or not you agree with it.

Most important, do I feel bad because I haven't accomplished enough? Achieved enough? Conformed enough? This is blackmail and antithetical to my philosophy. I must fight to give myself the right to feel good about myself and to feel good mood-wise, regardless of any accomplishment or nonaccomplishment whatsoever.[1]

I have heard leading Christian speakers say much the same

thing. I have read it in the writings of various authors. I personally must disagree, however, though I understand why it is said, and I sympathize with the intent.

I believe the statement expresses serious error, despite the fact that a correct concept underlies it. It is correct that we are of value apart from anything we do. We have essential worth as human beings. From the Christian perspective, we are of value as children of God and saints, as we discussed in chapter five. However, this concept is carried too far when the claim is made or the impression given that our performance should not affect our self-esteem at all.

Perhaps we have stumbled onto one reason self-esteem teachings sometimes don't "take." Counselors tell us our performance doesn't count, but though we want to believe that, a more convincing voice inside us says it *does* count. That voice is not simply the misguided teachings of their parents or the culture. It is, I believe, a voice from God.

The first thing God ever said to man was, "Be fruitful and increase in number; fill the earth and subdue it. Rule over . . . every living creature that moves on the ground" (Gen. 1:28).

This command identifies two of the most basic functions of man. The first is to reproduce (be fruitful, increase in number, fill the earth). The second is to achieve and exercise control over the earth.

Clearly, the first function relates to each of us personally and directly. We are sexual beings, and coming to terms with our sexuality in a positive, constructive way is essential to our well-being.

The second function relates to us in a similar fashion. We are achiever/manager beings. We need to be gaining control and exercising control over God's creation (see Ps. 8:3-8; Heb. 2:5-9).

When the Bible commands us to subdue and rule, it makes only one exception. We are not to dominate other people. Jesus was emphatic about that. He said: "You know that the rulers of the Gentiles lord it over them, and their high officials exercise authority over them. Not so with you. Instead, whoever wants to become great among you must be your servant" (Matt. 20:25,26).

Significantly, though, in the above passage, Jesus did not speak against wanting to "become great" when it's by serving people rather than using them. Self-realization is one thing, while dominating, using, intimidating, or exploiting people is quite another.

Psychologists talk about various kinds of behavior as different "social motivations," though their lists vary somewhat and so do their definitions of each motive. The desire to subdue and rule the creature universe, I identify with achievement motivation. The desire to dominate other people is a form of power motivation gone sour.

To return to our original agree/disagree statement, I maintain that we have an inner need to achieve because we were designed by God to be achievers. Therefore, we are not going to feel good about ourselves if we lack this essential component in our lives.

THE NONPRODUCTIVE LIFE

Jesus' parable of the barren fig tree has something to say to us on the question of performance. "A man had a fig tree, planted in his vineyard, and he went to look for fruit on it, but did not find any. So he said to the man who took care of the vineyard, 'For three years now I've been coming to look for fruit on this fig tree and haven't found any. Cut it down! Why should it use up the soil?'

" 'Sir,' the man replied, 'leave it alone for one more year, and I'll dig around it and fertilize it. If it bears fruit next year, fine! If not, then cut it down' " (Luke 13:6-9).

You and I are taking up space in God's vineyard, and he expects some "fruit" from us. Otherwise, why should he leave us here? By contrast, Dr. Wayne Dyer writes:

You exist. You are human. That is all you need. Your

131

worth is determined by you, and with no need for an explanation to anyone. And your worthiness, a given, has nothing to do with your behavior and feelings.[2]

There it is again. Performance is totally disallowed as affecting worth. But from a biblical viewpoint, it is *not* enough to know that you exist, that you are human. As the psalmist writes: "Know that the Lord is God. It is he who made us, and we are his, we are his people, the sheep of his pasture" (Ps. 100:3).

We are his people. He has a right to expect some return from us—and he does expect some return. Just what the "fruit" should be is another question. We don't all have to attain great things as men count greatness. Praise is fruit. Worship is fruit. But the principle remains: We are God's people living in God's world, and we need to be fruitful if we are to live at peace with ourselves and with him.

Let's be clear what we mean by achievement when we say achievement is for everyone.

SUCCESS IS NOT ENOUGH

A full-page ad in a major daily newspaper carries the bold headline: "The Lazy Man's Way to Riches." The copy proceeds to boast about the wealth of the man who placed the ad. He owns boats, mansions, beach properties, Cadillacs, stocks and bonds. He has money in the bank and plenty of leisure time. The ad concludes, "A month from today, you can be nothing more than thirty days older—or you can be on your way to getting rich."

Little kinship exists between a person who would grab for a "lazy man's way to riches" and an achiever. The ad virtually offers *success without achievement* and should be viewed with suspicion to say the least.

Scripture warns us that "people who want to get rich fall into temptation and a trap and into many foolish and harmful desires that plunge men into ruin and destruction. For the love of money is a root of all kinds of evil" (1 Tim. 6:9,10).

A tale is told of a young man encountering Satan. The two met on a hilltop early one morning. Satan, posing as a great benefactor, said, "Young man, I like you. I can see you have ambition and want to make the greatest possible success of your life. I want to help you. Look at this great land laying before us. I will give you, as a permanent possession, all of this land that you can cover by sundown tonight. But there is one condition: you must be back here by sundown, not one moment later."

The young man's heart leaped within him at the thought of such an opportunity, but he would be no fool. He must not try to encompass so much ground as to return late and forfeit everything. As he passed over the fertile lands and well-watered plains, he kept close track of the sun making its own circuit of the heavens. When it was directly overhead, he resolutely turned away from the land that alluringly beckoned him on and began the return leg of his journey.

All went well until the young man's steps took him past some springs bubbling from the ground, the stream flowing away into a sheltered cove just outside the area he was encompassing. *The perfect site for a home and fruit orchard, he thought. The one thing I'd need to make my holdings complete.* He looked at the sun still high in the afternoon sky, looked again at the Eden so close to being his, and altered his course.

The detour took longer than he expected, what with having to wade the stream. He'd need to hurry to make up the lost time. But he was weary now. It had been a long day and a very long journey. It hadn't even occurred to him that his strength might run out before his time did. He should have turned back before noon, he told himself; should have allowed longer for the return than for the journey out; should never have added that watercourse to his return trip.

He was struggling now, his feet heavy, his legs aching, his eyes watching, watching as the sun sank ever closer to the western horizon. And then at last he saw it. The hill! It loomed before him and on top of it stood the waiting figure of his benefactor.

133

His body told him to give up, that it was impossible. If he were fresh, he could sprint, and he just might make it. But he was exhausted. Silencing the cries of his tortured flesh, he broke into a run. The ground flew beneath his feet, but the sun seemed almost to match his pace in its plunge from the sky. *Faster, faster*, he ordered. His heart pounded furiously against his chest, and his circle of vision narrowed until only at the center was there light. He lurched forward until he collapsed finally at Satan's feet.

"Congratulations, young man, I see you've made it," Satan said as the edge of the burning red disc of the sun dropped from sight. The young man who lay crumpled at his feet didn't respond. "You shall have exactly what I promised," said Satan, "all the land you cover by sundown as a permanent possession." Then he laughed fiendishly. "I'd say you cover just about six feet." And they buried the young man there.[3]

"People who want to get rich fall into . . . a trap" (1 Tim. 6:9). That's one problem with "success motivation." It easily translates into greed or vanity. That's why I'm writing about achievement rather than about success. A person who aims at success is focused on the wrong thing, especially if his idea of success is to get rich.

GETTING THINGS DONE

One of the leading authorities in the study of achievement motivation is David C. McClelland, a Harvard psychologist. After reading others' reports of his work and after reading his book *The Achieving Society*, I telephoned McClelland to inquire about his views.

"Many people misunderstand what I mean by achievement," he told me. "Don't equate achievement motivation with success motivation. What I'm talking about might be called efficiency."

Later I found a similar definition in his book *Power, the Inner Experience*, in which he writes of achievement as "the satisfaction of doing a job well or efficiently, whether anyone else knows about it or not."

Exactly. Achievement relates to getting things done. Achievement is actual accomplishment, while success is an incidental result that sometimes follows.

You see, if a person does something—anything—particularly well, he is likely to gain money and recognition because of it. "Do you see a man skilled in his work? He will serve before kings; he will not serve before obscure men" (Prov. 22:29). His real credit, however, is in what he does, not in the success he enjoys as a result.

This is not to suggest that the achiever is totally indifferent to success. In most cases, he'd like it very much if his efforts were rewarded. Partly he likes money and recognition because they are pleasant to have, and partly he likes them because they are tangible evidences that he indeed is achieving something worthwhile. But his focus is on the achieving, not on the reward.

What we are saying, then, is this: success may or may not be God's will for you, but achievement *is* God's will. Achieving is not optional; it isn't only for the highly motivated. It isn't the private concern of those who are into some human potential or success movement.

Achievement is for you.

God made you that way.

If you're still not convinced, the direct command of the New Testament should help. I refer to Titus 3:14: "Our people must learn to devote themselves to doing what is good, in order that they may provide for daily necessities and not live unproductive lives."

As a Christian living in today's society, you have a concern that goes beyond simply providing your daily necessities. Welfare might do that. Begging might do it. Your concern is to lead a productive life—to get something worthwhile done.

The mischief in linking self-esteem with achievement comes when we fall into the trap of comparing our achievements with those of someone else. That is what is damaging and misguided.

My achievement has nothing to do with your achievement.

135

What may be a snap for you may be a real attainment for me. But while I do not need to match you, I do need my own sense of attainment.

As the Scripture says, "Each one should test his own actions. Then he can take pride in himself, without comparing himself to somebody else" (Gal. 6:4).

Yes, achievement is for everyone.

TIME TO CONSIDER

1. Some people are concerned with relationships but care little about achievement. Is this evidence of deficiency of character?

2. I wrote that God expects "fruit" from us, but praise and worship can constitute fruit (p. 132). Is that statement an attempt to accommodate the disabled, or is it really OK for an ordinary person to have no achievement goals?

3. Is it OK to have getting rich as a goal? Why or why not? What is the basic difference between working for achievement and working for success, prosperity, or recognition?

4. If achievement is desirable, why is it not good to esteem people on the basis of their performance: to view those who accomplish much as great, those who accomplish less as ordinary, and those who accomplish little as inferior?

12

...

Encouraging Achievement in Yourself and Others

How does one grow an achiever? If you want to make your life count but lack drive, can you do anything about it? If you want your children to be doers, actively seeking productive lives, is there any way you can encourage that?

To seek answers we could examine the lives of individuals who have achieved much and try to figure out what made them tick. The trouble is we would have little idea how much their achievement depended on motivational principles we observe and how much resulted from their own unique combination of gifts and opportunities.

There is another approach. We can look at some great societies. When a people as a whole register impressive achievement, it seems pretty clear they must be doing something right.

WHAT MADE THEM GREAT?

Many theories have been advanced to explain the rise and fall of great societies. Unfortunately, Christians have sometimes been preoccupied with the "decline" side of the ledger. We see what happened to the Roman Empire or to the cities of Sodom and Gomorrah, and we warn of dangerous parallels in our own culture. As valid as that may be, it can produce a decline-and-fall mentality. Instead of producing anything positive, we get caught up in trying to slow the processes of degeneration. We become mere reactors to existing conditions instead of initiators of good. That's not a desirable pattern for us when we speak in the name of the Creator.

Before a society ever declined and fell, it first had to rise. We should ask what made it rise. One theory for explaining the rise of a great culture is basically racist. For example, blacks supposedly could never build a great civilization because they were slave-caliber people, and regardless of their social or legal status, that was all one could ever expect of them.

The racist view of societies has taken many forms. Some have been sinister and murderous, like Hitler's. He was ready to kill millions of Jews and other "inferiors" in the interests of an Aryan super race.

Other forms of racism have been seemingly innocuous—like the claim that Nordic people have influenced the rise of most great civilizations. Then there are the amusing variations such as Fanfani's claim that people with long heads make the best businessmen.

Since we can do nothing about our racial origins, and little about the shape of our heads, these theories seem more useful for giving people excuses than anything else. They give the unmotivated an excuse to stagnate and the exploiters an excuse to ride over others.

Another widely-held view, best advanced by the Yale geographer Ellsworth Huntington, is that climate determines the vigor and greatness of a society. In his book *Civilization and*

Climate, published in 1915, Huntington pointed out that no great civilization has ever flourished in either the arctic zones or the tropics. Presumably survival is such a struggle in frigid climates that the people have little time for anything more. In the tropics, it's just too hot to think or work very much.

Huntington plotted in detail the exact temperature variations needed for optimum human development and the areas of the globe where such a climate prevails. If you think he was right, you may want to move your place of residence accordingly.

However, while climate can no doubt encourage or limit achievement, it seems clear that it cannot cause it. After all, the nations in Huntington's ideal climates vary widely in achievement. For that matter, a nation may change greatly over a relatively short period of time while its climate remains the same. Obviously, something more than climate is involved. I believe the major factor is psychological.

Whether you want to change your place of residence or not, you might try changing your attitude. That sounds simple, though not always easy. Is there evidence it would do any good? Yes.

Substantial historical evidence supports the view that achievement does not depend so much on various fortuitous circumstances as on psychological orientation. In other words, *people who want to achieve and who think of themselves as achievers really do get things done.*

David C. McClelland's studies (see previous chapter) of great societies past and present indicate that *before* a given culture reached its peak, achievement motivation was high. For example, for two hundred years before the Golden Age of Pericles—the fifth century B.C., when Athenian culture was at its peak and the wonders of the Acropolis were built—achievement themes were prominent in the speeches, orations, dramas, poems, and other literature. By the time the culture reached its zenith, achievement motivation had gone into decline. The culture soon followed.

This pattern appears not only in ancient Athens but in

contemporary cultures worldwide. The rise and fall of motivation *precedes* the rise and fall of achievement.

This should come as good news to us because it means we can accomplish things once we find ways to turn on our "want to."

Now we come to the real issue. What specific, practical actions can a person take to stimulate a desire to achieve, in himself or others? I suggest four possibilities.

1. *To develop achievement motivation, one should read extensively in achievement-oriented literature.* It matters what we read. If I didn't believe that, I wouldn't waste my time writing. I believe this book can and will change lives. I know my own life has been influenced, sometimes decisively, by what I have read.

I'm not suggesting, however, that you concentrate your reading on popular psychology or self-help books. Contemporary literature rich in achievement motivation ranges from delightful children's stories such as *The Little Engine That Could* and *Abel's Island* to the biographies of George Washington Carver and Helen Keller. From *Profiles in Courage* to *Roots* to *The Incredible Journey.*

I am concerned, however, with what a comparison of our present literary and television/movie diet with that of a generation ago might show. I would guess we'd see a frightening decline in the achievement content. The old-time hero who prevailed against overwhelming odds has in many cases been replaced by a somewhat dissolute, easygoing character who is the victim of a corrupt system.

Fortunately, one great source of achievement-oriented reading—the source that probably most influenced achievers of the past and present—is still available to us. I refer to the Bible. What towering examples of achievement in the face of adversity we find there! We read of:

- Noah, who built a great lifeboat though he had to work for one hundred twenty years under the derisive gaze of his contemporaries to do it;
- Abraham, who left the security of Ur to pioneer and claim

an uncharted wilderness;

- Joseph, a forgotten man in prison in a foreign land, who rose to become governor of that land;
- Moses, who defied the wrath of Pharaoh and led an army of malcontents through a forty-year trek in the wilderness to make them a nation;
- Gideon, the "loaf of barley bread," who routed an army of one hundred thirty-five thousand men with a band of three hundred;
- the tragic Samson, who killed more enemies of the Lord at his death than he did during his lifetime;
- David, venturing out against the fearful giant Goliath and returning the victor;
- Daniel, coming out of a den of lions—alive—so that a pagan king proclaimed the God of Daniel to be supreme over all.

When Scripture lists the greatest heroes of all time, it talks largely of achievement, of those who "through faith conquered kingdoms, administered justice, and gained what was promised; who shut the mouths of lions, quenched the fury of the flames, and escaped the edge of the sword; whose weakness was turned to strength; and who became powerful in battle and routed foreign armies" (Heb. 11:33,34).

Jesus himself is presented in Scripture as a man with a goal to achieve. He told his disciples, "My food is to do the will of him who sent me and to finish his work" (John 4:34). Another time he said, "I have a baptism to undergo, and how distressed I am until it is completed!" (Luke 12:50).

The writer to the Hebrews says that Jesus "for the joy set before him endured the cross, scorning its shame, and sat down at the right hand of the throne of God" (Heb. 12:2). I would not trivialize his great sacrifice by comparing it with our ventures. His is the all-surpassing achievement. Yet we, like our Lord, will endure whatever it takes to achieve our ends if the joy of doing so is set vividly before us.

One way to set the joy of achievement before us is to read of others' triumphs. Yes, if you want to become an achiever, read achievement-oriented literature. Read the Bible. Doing so could be one reason so many people with evangelical roots have excelled in all walks of life.

2. *To become an achiever, affiliate with a church that encourages independent devotion and personal responsibility before God.* McClelland writes:

> It may be concluded with reasonable confidence that, as of 1950, Protestant countries are economically more advanced on the average, even taking their differences in natural resources into account, than are Catholic countries.[1]

A consistent pattern appears historically for members of certain Protestant sects (Quakers, Anabaptists, Methodists) to show remarkable enterprise. All of these sects in their early days were "ultra-protestant" in the sense of strongly rejecting traditional church authority and stressing the individual's direct communion with God.

One might ask whether this religious individualism really produced achievers or whether the two traits just happened to coincide. Striking evidence that the former is the case comes from the other great religions of the world.

Among the Hindus of north India, for example, a Vaishnava sect—which claims that worship by lay people in their homes is as valid as worship led by a priest in the temple—is conspicuously successful in business compared to other Hindus. McClelland writes:

> The number of similar cases could be multiplied; the rise of the business class in Japan in the 19th century was associated with a special form of Buddhism—Zen, which again is a form of positive mysticism which is definitely individualistic and against many ritual forms.[2]

As one last example, McClelland cites the Jews:

> It is a curious fact that the distinct business success of Jews within the past few generations has been associated with a strong antirabbinical mystical movement within Judaism known as Hassidism ... an attempt to escape from "formalism and ecclesiastical systems" and to encourage the believer to feel that he could directly and joyously feel the presence of God.[3]

In an interesting test of his theories, McClelland matched two Mexican villages, one a traditional Catholic village and one that had been converted to Protestantism. He found that the Protestants were generally higher in achievement motivation than were their Catholic counterparts. (He also found a much wider variation among the Protestants; they had a few individuals who tested highest and a few who tested lowest.)

Today, one certainly cannot assume that every fellowship of Protestants will encourage individualism and that every Catholic church will be tradition-bound. What one *can* assume is that any church, whatever its label, that exalts formal, ritualistic religion above a direct, personal relationship with God does so to the detriment of its members' achievement motivation. To say nothing of their spiritual welfare.

3. *To help your children become achievers, encourage self-reliance in them at an early age.* What characterizes the relationships between parents and their children in homes that produce the highest achievers? Researchers have sought answers to that question.

Marian R. Winterbottom, and many others after her, found that a mother's attitude in bringing up her children has a significant effect on their achievement motivation. Winterbottom sought to determine at what ages children were expected to learn self-reliance in such matters as:

- feeding themselves without help;
- undressing and preparing for bed;

- taking care of toys and clothes;
- doing assigned household chores;
- playing in the neighborhood outside their yards;
- making their own friends;
- deciding how to spend their own money;
- entertaining themselves;
- doing well in competition.

Winterbottom discovered that sons whose mothers expected self-reliance of them at relatively early ages rated high in achievement motivation. Sons kept dependent on their parents characteristically were less interested in achievement.

Subsequent testing by other researchers supported these conclusions but with some significant modifications. It seems that the *reason* a mother demands self-reliance in her children is important. If she "abandons" the child to care for himself so that she won't have to be bothered or because she is simply careless and indifferent, no positive effect on the child's desire for achievement follows. The mother needs to be warmly involved with her children, supporting them, and praising their accomplishments. She also needs to be a person of reasonably high standards and expectations herself.

A father can also have a significant effect on his child's achievement motivation. Dominating fathers who tell their children exactly what to do and how to do it rather than letting them function on their own with only minimum necessary guidance tend to produce underachievers. This may explain why strong fathers so often produce weak sons.

That pattern is not unavoidable. Many strong fathers are wise enough to give their children room to grow. Others may be so busily occupied with their own exploits that their children escape their close supervision. In either case, the child may do well, though in one case it is because of the father's virtues and in the other despite his neglect. Anyhow, the strong father who is closely involved with his children needs to be careful not to dominate them because his natural instincts will no doubt run that way.

Scripture says, "It is good for a man to bear the yoke while he is young" (Lam. 3:27). That seems to be another way of saying: train your children early in self-reliance.

4. *To become an achiever despite any disadvantages from your past, repent and believe the Scriptures.* Your parents may not have encouraged self-reliance in you at an early age. Your church background may not have been stimulating to your individual initiative. You may not have been raised on a diet of stories of great achievers. As a result, you may be disadvantaged, but *you are not disqualified.*

No one has an ideal background. That's why we all need the grace of God. We live in a fallen world. Our parents and others who have influenced our lives are all imperfect. It would be foolish to argue that undesirable influences have had no effect on us. They have. But what we become does not have to be determined by these powerful forces from the past. The grace of God can make a difference. God the Creator can work creatively in us. He will as we trust him to do so.

First, though, a person must clarify his concept of what he should do and be. How can you ask God to change your life if you don't know what changes are needed?

We've come full circle in this section. We cited the command of God to subdue and rule the earth. We said that means each of us should become an achiever. Jesus had something to say on the same subject in the form of a parable:

"A man going on a journey . . . called his servants and entrusted his property to them. To one he gave five talents of money, to another two talents, and to another one talent, each according to his ability. Then he went on his journey. The man who had received the five talents went at once and put his money to work and gained five more. So also, the one with the two talents gained two more. But the man who had received the one talent went off, dug a hole in the ground and hid his master's money.

"After a long time the master of those servants returned

and settled accounts with them. The man who had received the five talents brought the other five. 'Master,' he said, 'you entrusted me with five talents. See, I have gained five more.'

"His master replied, 'Well done, good and faithful servant! You have been faithful with a few things; I will put you in charge of many things. Come and share your master's happiness!'

"The man with two talents also came. 'Master,' he said, 'you entrusted me with two talents; see, I have gained two more.'

"His master replied, 'Well done, good and faithful servant! You have been faithful with a few things; I will put you in charge of many things. Come and share your master's happiness!'

Then the man who had received the one talent came. 'Master,' he said, 'I knew that you are a hard man, harvesting where you have not sown and gathering where you have not scattered seed. So I was afraid and went out and hid your talent in the ground. See, here is what belongs to you.'

"His master replied, 'You wicked, lazy servant! So you knew that I harvest where I have not sown and gather where I have not scattered seed? Well then, you should have put my money on deposit with the bankers so that when I returned I would have received it back with interest' " (Matt. 25:14-27).

Notice that the parable describes the ways in which three different people use the resources entrusted to them. Two invest their money, double it, and receive commendation and increased opportunity. The third person buries his and seems to argue that he has done well to break even. For this, he is severely reprimanded.

An important question: what motivated the third man? He said, "I was afraid, and went out and hid your talent" (v. 25).

I was afraid. Certainly one of the chief enemies of achievement is fear of failure. Ironically, the man who feared failure in the parable is the only one who experienced it. You see, fear of failure does nothing to lessen the likelihood of failure and in fact tends to assure it by incapacitating a person. If you are paralyzed by fear or struggling with it, read the previous section of this book again, and especially chapter nine.

But why was the man in the parable afraid? He said to his master, "I knew that you are a hard man, harvesting where you have not sown . . . so I was afraid" (vv. 24,25).

Wasn't that irrational? If the master were so adept at making everything turn a profit, why did not this man, in effect a partner of the master, expect happy results? Apparently, he saw himself more as a potential victim of the master than as a partner.

This man represents the person who has a negative view of God and the world. God is a "hard man," and this world he has placed us in eats up its inhabitants. One does well to hold his own in this fearful place, let alone gain anything. And God is a rigorous Judge who will not brook any failure.

So, then, the fear of the non-achiever betrays the fact that he has a spiritual problem. Thus the master says, "You wicked, lazy servant!" (v. 26). In the master's judgment, this man's inactivity reveals a moral flaw, not just an unfortunate choice. The man was *wicked*.

When was the last time you heard a sermon on the wickedness of not developing your achievement potential? Preachers have called many things sinful—too often things that the Bible never so designates—but too few call this dereliction of duty *wicked*, as the Lord does.

Even though you may not hear this preached much, it is by no means a novel idea. Sloth traditionally has been recognized by the church as one of the seven deadly sins. That's why this fourth principle for encouraging achievement motivation is *repent and believe the Scriptures*. God can certainly give you grace to accomplish many worthwhile things during your lifetime, but first you must realize he expects you to do exactly that.

147

Now it's your move. Get started, and God will be with you.

Say, did you notice what was *missing* from the parable? We saw servants who set out to accomplish something and did. We saw a servant who held back and was condemned. But we didn't see anyone who ventured out and failed.

How come? Because there is no such thing.

No such thing as venturing out and failing? That certainly cannot be true.

Right. What we're saying is that anyone who consistently seeks to develop and use his potential will not fail in the long run. Some of his projects may fail, but *he* won't. Furthermore, his failures will be only preliminary to the ultimate achievement of worthwhile goals.

One of my favorite Scriptures puts it this way: "Sow your seed in the morning, and at evening let not your hands be idle, for you do now know which will succeed, whether this or that, or whether both will do equally well" (Eccl. 11:6).

Note the possibilities. Maybe morning sowing will succeed. Maybe evening sowing. Maybe both. What is not mentioned? *Maybe neither.*

Like Jesus' parable of the talents, this verse allows for no such thing as ultimate failure for the consistent sower. So seize your opportunities. You don't know which of your efforts will bear fruit, but some will. You may be happily surprised to find some day that they all did.

TIME TO CONSIDER

1. When a child says, "See what I can do?" and performs some act which he expects you to applaud, should you:

    a. encourage the child

    b. correct the child

    c. ignore the child

Would the same basic principle apply to adults?

2. How does reading the Bible help motivate us toward

meaningful action and achievement?

3. How does your own experience confirm or contradict the studies that claim achievement motivation is fostered by:
   a. attending a church that stresses individuality
   b. having parents who encourage early self-reliance

4. How does fear of failure tend to cause failure? How is inaction that stems from fear of failure inconsistent with a correct view of God?

5. Three words used to describe the unprofitable servant in the parable of the talents are *afraid*, *wicked*, and *lazy*. To what degree does each of these (fear, wickedness, laziness) hinder you from stepping out and taking action? What assurance from God, when believed, will free us from the fear of failure?

6. What important lasting insights have you gained from this book? Are you replacing any wrong ways of thinking with new thoughts and attitudes? If so, give examples. What vision for your life do you now embrace as relates to your self-concept? Where are you headed?

Source Notes

Introduction

1. "If You Want Joy" by Joseph D. Carlson.

Chapter 1

1. Jerry Cook with Stanley C. Baldwin, *Love, Acceptance, and Forgiveness* (Ventura, CA: Regal Books, 1979), p. 88.
2. Ibid., p. 88.

Chapter 3

1. Robert H. Schuller, *Self-Love: The Dynamic Source of Success* (Old Tappan, NJ: Fleming H. Revell Co., 1969).
2. The group identity phenomenon shows itself curiously in professional sports. When a team gains a world championship, people from the city the team represents go wild. Even many with little interest in the game get caught up in the

excitement. The players, however, are usually not "our local boys" at all. They were recruited from far and near, simply hired for the job, and in coming seasons will likely play for opposing teams. Nevertheless, just because they represent a certain city and are winning, the locals feel great pride.

Chapter 5

1. Stanley C. Baldwin, *When Death Means Life: Choosing the Way of the Cross*, (Portland, OR: Multnomah Press, 1986), p. 128.
2. Ibid., p. 129.
3. Jerry Cook with Stanley C. Baldwin, *A Few Things I've Learned Since I Knew It All*, (Dallas, TX: Word, 1989), pp. 144, 145.
4. James D. Mallory, Jr. with Stanley C. Baldwin, *The Kink and I* (Wheaton, IL: Scripture Press Publications, 1973), p. 79.

Chapter 6

1. Norman M. Lobsenz, "How to Give and Get More Emotional Support," Women's Day, September 20, 1977, pp. 73,148,150.
2. Adapted by permission from *Free Way* (Wheaton, IL: Scripture Press Publications, Inc. 1973).
3. Jane Merchant, "Purchase," in *The Greatest of These* (Nashville: Abingdon Press, 1954). Used by permission.

Chapter 7

1. James D. Mallory, Jr. with Stanley C. Baldwin, *The Kink and I* (Wheaton, IL: Scripture Press Publications, Inc., 1973), pp. 179,180.

Chapter 8

1. Adapted from Dale Galloway's *How to Feel Like a Somebody Again* (Eugene, OR: Harvest House Publishers, 1978).

2. Bruce Narramore and Bill Counts, *Guilt and Freedom* (Santa Ana, CA: Vision House Publishers), pp. 124, 125.
3. For an in-depth theological treatment of this theme see David C. Needham, *Birthright* (Portland, OR: Multnomah Press).
4. Dr. James Dobson, *Emotions: Can You Trust Them?* (Ventura, CA: Regal Books, 1980), p. 22.
5. Stanley C. Baldwin, *When Death Means Life* (Portland, OR: Multnomah Press, 1986) pp. 125, 126.
6. Narramore and Counts, *Guilt and Freedom*, pp. 79-81.

Chapter 9

1. Craig Selness, *From Frustration to Fulfillment* (Wheaton, IL: SP Publications, Inc. 1982).
2. Samuel Scoville Jr., *"The Last Lap,"* Sunday School Times.

Chapter 10

1. John Powell, S.J., *Unconditional Love* (Niles, IL: Argus Communications, 1978). p. 69.
2. Ibid., p. 56.
3. Sharon Johnson, from an unpublished manuscript 1981 by Sharon Johnson.
4. Wayne W. Dyer, *Pulling Your Own Strings* (New York: Thomas Y. Crowell Co., 1978), pp. 126,127.
5. Powell, *Unconditional Love*, pp. 114-116.

Chapter 11

1. Dr. Theodore Isaac Rubin, *Compassion and Self-Hate* (New York: David McKay Co., 1975), p. 183.
2. Wayne W. Dyer, *Your Erroneous Zones* (New York: Thomas Y. Crowell Co., 1976), p. 43.
3. Adapted from Leo Tolstoy, *"How Much Land Does a Man Need?"*

Chapter 12

1. D.C. McClelland, *The Achieving Society* (Princeton: D. Van Nostrand Co., 1961), p. 53.
2. Ibid., p. 369.
3. Ibid., p. 370.

Stanley C. Baldwin offers seminars and meetings on these principles to groups across the United States and Canada. If you want him to come to your area, or if you want information on scheduling a seminar, write:

SBM, Inc.
P.O. Box 101
Oregon City, OR 97045

Support Group Leader's Guide

Issue-oriented, problem-wrestling, life-confronting—Heart Issue books are appropriate for adult Sunday school classes, individual study, and especially for support groups. Here are guidelines to encourage and facilitate support groups.

SUPPORT GROUP GUIDELINES

The small group setting offers individuals the opportunity to commit themselves to personal growth through mutual caring and support. This is especially true of Christian support groups, where from five to twelve individuals meet on a regular basis with a mature leader to share their personal experiences and struggles over a specific "heart issue." In such a group, individuals develop trust and accountability with each other and the Lord. Because a support group's purpose differs from a Bible study or prayer group, it needs its own format and guidelines.

Let's look at the ingredients of a support group:
- Purpose
- Leadership
- Meeting Format
- Group Guidelines

PURPOSE

The purpose of a Heart Issue support group is to provide:

1. An *opportunity* for participants to share openly and honestly their struggles and pain over a specific issue in a non-judgmental, Christ-centered framework.

2. A *"safe place"* where participants can gain perspective on a mutual problem and begin taking responsibility for their responses to their own situations.

3. An *atmosphere* that is compassionate, understanding, and committed to challenging participants from a biblical perspective.

Support groups are not counseling groups. Participants come to be supported, not fixed or changed. Yet, as genuine love and caring are exchanged, people begin to experience God's love and acceptance. As a result, change and healing take place.

The initiators of a support group need to be clear about its specific purpose. The following questions are examples of what to consider before starting a small group.

1. What type of group will this be? A personal growth group, a self-help group, or a group structured to focus on a certain theme? Is it long-term, short-term, or ongoing?

2. Who is the group for? A particular population? College students? Single women? Divorced people?

3. What are the goals for the group? What will members gain from it?

4. Who will lead or co-lead the group? What are his/her qualifications?

5. How many members should be in the group? Will new members be able to join the group once it is started?

6. What kind of structure or format will the group have?

7. What topics will be explored in the support book and to what degree will this be determined by the group members and to what degree by the leaders?

LEADERSHIP

Small group studies often rotate leadership among participants, but because support groups usually meet for a specific time period with a specific mutual issue, it works well to have one leader or a team of co-leaders responsible for the meetings.

Good leadership is essential for a healthy, balanced group. Qualifications include character and personality traits as well as life experience and, in some cases, professional experience.

Personal Leadership Characteristics

COURAGE

One of the most important traits of effective group leaders is courage. Courage is shown in willingness (1) to be open to self-disclosure, admitting their own mistakes and taking the same risks they expect others to take; (2) to confront another, and, in confronting, to understand that love is the goal; (3) to act on their beliefs and hunches; (4) to be emotionally touched by another and to draw on their experiences in order to identify with the other; (5) to continually examine their inner self; (6) to be direct and honest with members; and (7) to express to the group their fears and expectations about the group process. (Leaders shouldn't use their role to protect themselves from honest and direct interaction with the rest of the group.)

WILLINGNESS TO MODEL

Through their behavior, and the attitudes conveyed by it, leaders can create a climate of openness, seriousness of purpose, acceptance of others, and the desirability of taking risks. Group leaders should have had some moderate victory in their own struggles, with adequate healing having taken place. They recognize their own woundedness and see themselves as persons in

159

process as well. Group leaders lead largely by example—by doing what they expect members to do.

PRESENCE

Group leaders need to be emotionally present with the group members. This means being touched by others' pain, struggles, and joys. Leaders can become more emotionally involved with others by paying close attention to their own reactions and by permitting these reactions to become intense. Fully experiencing emotions gives leaders the ability to be compassionate and empathetic with their members. At the same time, group leaders understand their role as facilitators. They know they're not answer people; they don't take responsibility for change in others.

GOODWILL AND CARING

A sincere interest in the welfare of the others is essential in group leaders. Caring involves respecting, trusting, and valuing people. Not every member is easy to care for, but leaders should at least want to care. It is vital that leaders become aware of the kinds of people they care for easily and the kinds they find it difficult to care for. They can gain this awareness by openly exploring their reactions to members. Genuine caring must be demonstrated; merely saying so is not enough.

Some ways to express a caring attitude are: (1) inviting a person to participate but allowing that person to decide how far to go; (2) giving warmth, concern, and support when, and only when it is genuinely felt; (3) gently confronting the person when there are obvious discrepancies between a person's words and her behavior; and (4) encouraging people to be what they could be without their masks and shields. This kind of caring requires a commitment to love and a sensitivity to the Holy Spirit.

OPENNESS

To be effective, group leaders must be open with themselves, open to others in groups, open to new experiences, and open to life-styles and values that differ from their own. Openness is an attitude. It doesn't mean that leaders reveal every aspect of their personal lives; it means that they reveal enough of themselves to give the participants a sense of person.

Leader openness tends to foster a spirit of openness within the group; it permits members to become more open about their feelings and beliefs; and it lends a certain fluidity to the group process. Self-revelation should not be manipulated as a technique. However, self-evaluation is best done spontaneously, when appropriate.

NONDEFENSIVENESS

Dealing frankly with criticism is related closely to openness. If group leaders are easily threatened, insecure in their work of leading, overly sensitive to negative feedback, and depend highly on group approval, they will probably encounter major problems in trying to carry out their leadership role. Members sometimes accuse leaders of not caring enough, of being selective in their caring, of structuring the sessions too much, of not providing enough direction, of being too harsh. Some criticism may be fair, some unfair. The crucial thing for leaders is to nondefensively explore with their groups the feelings that are legitimately produced by the leaders and those that represent what is upsetting the member.

STRONG SENSE OF SELF

A strong sense of self (or personal power) is an important quality of leaders. This doesn't mean that leaders would manipulate or dominate; it means that leaders are confident of who they are and what they are about. Groups "catch" this and feel the leaders know what they are doing. Leaders who have a strong sense of self recognize their weaknesses and don't expend energy concealing them from others. Their vulnerability becomes their strength as leaders. Such leaders can accept credit where it's due, and at the same time encourage members to accept credit for their own growth.

STAMINA

Group leading can be taxing and draining as well as exciting and energizing. Leaders need physical and emotional stamina and the ability to withstand pressure in order to remain vitalized until the group sessions end. If leaders give in to fatigue when the group bogs down, becomes resistive, or when members drop out, the effectiveness of the whole group could suffer. Leaders must be aware of their own energy level, have outside sources of spiritual and emotional nourishment, and have realistic expectations for the group's progress.

SENSE OF HUMOR

The leaders who enjoy humor and can incorporate it appropriately into the group will bring a valuable asset to the meetings. Sometimes humor surfaces as an escape from healthy confrontations and sensitive leaders need to identify and help the group avoid this diversion. But because we often take ourselves and our problems so seriously, we need the release of humor to bring balance and perspective. This is particularly true after sustained periods of dealing seriously with intensive problems.

CREATIVITY

The capacity to be spontaneously creative, to approach each group session with fresh ideas is a most important characteristic for group leaders. Leaders who are good at discovering new ways of approaching a group and who are willing to suspend the use of established techniques are unlikely to grow stale. Working with interesting co-leaders is another way for leaders to acquire fresh ideas.

GROUP LEADERSHIP SKILLS

Although personality characteristics of the group leader are extremely significant, by themselves they do not insure a healthy group. Leadership skills are also essential. The following need to be expressed in a sensitive and timely way:

ACTIVE LISTENING

Leaders need to absorb content, note gestures, observe subtle changes in voice or expression, and sense underlying messages. For example, a woman may be talking about her warm and loving feelings toward her husband, yet her body may be rigid and her fists clenched.

EMPATHY

This requires sensing the subjective world of the participant. Group leaders, in addition to being caring and open, must learn to grasp another's experience and at the same time maintain their separateness.

RESPECT AND POSITIVE REGARD

In giving support, leaders need to draw on the positive assets of the members. Where differences occur, there needs to be open and honest appreciation and toleration.

WARMTH

Smiling has been shown to be especially important in the communication of warmth. Other nonverbal means are: voice tone, posture, body language, and facial expression.

GENUINENESS

Leaders need to be real, to be themselves in relating with others, to be authentic and spontaneous.

FORMAT

The format of meetings will differ vastly from group to group, but the following are generally accepted as working well with support groups.

MEETING PLACE

This should be a comfortable, warm atmosphere. Participants need to feel welcome and that they've come to a "safe place" where they won't be overheard or easily distracted. Some groups will want to provide baby-sitting.

OPENING

Welcome participants. The leader should introduce herself and the members should also introduce themselves. It is wise to go over the "ground rules" at every meeting and especially at first or when there are newcomers. Some of these would include:

1. Respect others' sharing by keeping what is said in the group confidential.

2. Never belittle the beliefs or expressions of another.

3. Respect the time schedule. Try to arrive on time and be prompt in leaving.

4. Feel free to contact the leader at another time if there are questions or need for additional help.

Many meetings open with a brief time of prayer and worship and conclude with prayer. It often helps to ask for informal prayer requests and brief sharing so that the group begins in a spirit of openness.

MEETING

Leaders can initiate the meeting by focusing on a particular issue (or chapter if the group is studying a book). It is wise to define the focus of the specific meeting so that the group can stay on track for the entire session. (See Group Guidelines below.)

CLOSING

Strive for promptness without being abrupt. Give opportunity for those who need additional help to make an appointment with the leader. Be alert to any needing special affirmation or encouragement as they leave.

GROUP GUIDELINES

Because this is a support group, not an advice group, the leader will need to establish the atmosphere and show by her style how to relate lovingly and helpfully within the group. Participants need to know the guidelines for being a member of the group. It is a wise practice to repeat these guidelines at each meeting and especially when newcomers attend. The following guidelines have proven to be helpful to share with support groups:

1. You have come to give and receive support. No "fixing." We are to listen, support, and be supported by one another—not give advice.

2. Let other members talk. Please let them finish without interruption.

3. Try to step over any fear of sharing in the group. Yet do not

monopolize the group's time.

4. Be interested in what someone else is sharing. Listen with your heart. Never converse privately with someone else while another member is addressing the group.

5. Be committed to express your feelings from the heart. Encourage others to do the same. It's all right to feel angry, to laugh, or to cry.

6. Help others own their feelings and take responsibility for change in their lives. Don't jump in with an easy answer or a story on how you conquered their problem. Relate to where they are.

7. Avoid accusing or blaming. Speak in the "I" mode about how something or someone made *you* feel. Example: "I felt angry when. . . ."

8. Avoid ill-timed humor to lighten emotionally charged times. Let participants work through their sharing even if it is hard.

9. Keep names and sharing of other group members confidential.

10. Because we are all in various stages of growth, please give newcomers permission to be new and old-timers permission to be further along in their growth. This is a "safe place" for all to grow and share their lives.